Supporting Every Child's Learning

across the **Early Years Foundation Stage**

Vicky Hutchin

HODDER
EDUCATION
PART OF HACHETTE LIVRE UK

'Let children be children. A skilled five year old grows from a busy four year old, a curious three year old, a cuddled two year old, an adventurous one year old and a communicative baby.'

'Learning Together', *Early Education*

Also by Vicky Hutchin:

Observing and Assessing for the Foundation Stage Profile

Right from the Start

Tracking Significant Achievement in the Early Years

Although every effort has been made to ensure that website addresses are correct at time of going to press, Hodder Education cannot be held responsible for the content of any website mentioned in this book. It is sometimes possible to find a relocated web page by typing in the address of the home page for a website in the URL window of your browser.

Hachette's policy is to use papers that are natural, renewable and recyclable products and made from wood grown in sustainable forests. The logging and manufacturing processes are expected to conform to the environmental regulations of the country of origin.

Orders: please contact Bookpoint Ltd, 130 Milton Park, Abingdon, Oxon OX14 4SB. Telephone: (44) 01235 827720. Fax: (44) 01235 400454. Lines are open 9.00–5.00, Monday to Saturday, with a 24-hour message answering service. Visit our website at www.hoddereducation.co.uk

Cover photos: Boy Playing with Building Blocks © Dex Images/CORBIS; Boy playing in a puddle © Ariel Skelley/CORBIS; all other photos by Billy Ridgers.

Typeset by Servis Filmsetting Ltd, Manchester.
Printed in Great Britain by Martins the Printers, Berwick upon Tweed

A catalogue record for this title is available from the British Library

ISBN 978 0 340 94777 7

Contents

Acknowledgements

I wish to thank all the children, parents and practitioners who contributed to this book, from: Fortune Park Children's Centre, Bond Primary School Foundation Stage Unit, St Saviour's CE Infants School, Tunstall Children's Centre and Nutfield Day Nursery.

A very special thanks to the following parents, practitioners and heads: Caron Rudge, Sandy Gizzi, Jan Peek, Lisa Francis, Angela O'Connor, Julia Barry, Janet Harper, Ed Harker, Penny Nicholls and team, Sue Hirscheimer, Ally Bertin and team, Nina Simoes and Oscar Salgado, Alice Chan, Chris and Katie Ridgers, and Emma and Kevin Elliott.

A mention too goes to Sally Jaeckle, and to Kieran Gallagher who helped ensure I took at least a little exercise during the writing of this book. And in particular, many thanks to Billy Ridgers for his patient help, for looking after me while I was busy writing and for lots of the photographs in this book.

Vicky Hutchin

Introduction

Recent developments in UK government policy for early years provision have resulted in new expectations and requirements for all those working right across the early years, from birth upwards to nearly six years old. In 2000, for the first time in England, a comprehensive curriculum guidance aimed at those working with three, four and five year olds was published: the *Curriculum Guidance for the Foundation Stage*. It became the statutory document for all Foundation Stage settings in the maintained and private, voluntary and independent sectors. In 2003, the *Birth to Three Matters Framework* was also published to support those working with children up to the age of three. In 2007, a new statutory document, the *Early Years Foundation Stage* (EYFS), consolidated both within one single framework. Although this new framework builds on what was already in place, there are major implications for what all practitioners do to ensure they support *every* child to learn and develop. This book is designed to help you, whatever your current role.

> The EYFS pack is made up of the Statutory Framework and Practice Guidance booklets, Principles into Practice cards, Wall Poster and CD-ROM. It is available to download from two websites: www.everychildmatters.gov.uk and www.teachernet.gov.uk/publications . A wide variety of documents relevant to early childhood education and care are on the CD-ROM. Many are referred to in the text of this book.

Across the age range

The book offers practical support, advice and guidance, with many real examples of what practitioners and settings are doing now, particularly relating to their observation, assessment and planning processes. It draws on the approaches taken in two previous books: *Right from the Start: Effective Planning and Assessment* (Hutchin, 1999) and *Observing and Assessing for the Foundation Stage Profile* (Hutchin,

2003). But most significantly it looks at the *full* age range, from the youngest months to when a child starts school in Year 1, at the age of five and, for some, nearly six years.

Most providers take children for only a part of the age range covered by the EYFS: only a very few settings cover the complete age range. Playgroups and preschools tend to take children from the age of two to three or four, nursery classes take three and four year olds, whereas day nurseries and children's centres take children from a few months to age four or nearly five. For children's centres, this is in addition to a range of services for parents, such as parent and toddler 'stay and play' sessions. Reception classes take the oldest in the age range, and nearly all children start school before statutory school age (which is the term after the child's fifth birthday). To add to this profusion of services, there are a myriad of terms used to describe the different settings! These complex patterns of provision mean that transition between settings is important to get right, to ensure it is as smooth and seamless as possible.

A consistent approach

Concerns are often voiced about the amount of paperwork that record keeping and planning generates. However, the real issue is not about the *amount* of observations, assessments and planning sheets you have, but about ensuring what you write is truly useful in supporting the children's development. The examples, advice and guidance in this book show how a *similar approach* to assessment and planning is needed across the age group and types of settings, appropriately tailored to the children, thus enabling smooth transitions to take place. The emphasis in the EYFS on the 'Unique Individual' and 'Meeting Diverse Needs' can seem complex when planning for a whole group of children, some of whom may not be in your setting for very long. Practitioners also change the age group and type of setting with which they work, so having a consistent approach to observing, assessing and planning is vital, and now fully supported by the EYFS.

The consultation draft of the EYFS published in Summer 2006 stated that '*All children should have a development and learning record to which parents and practitioners contribute and which will go with them from setting to setting*' (DfES, 2006a). Even though this statement was not included in the final, published EYFS documents, we know in principle that this is in every child's best interests and we should all be working towards it. There is still very strong advice in the final EYFS statutory guidance:

' Assessments should be based on practitioners' observation of what children are doing in their day-to-day activities. . . . it is expected that all adults who interact with the child should contribute to the process . . . . '

Starting with the children

Effective planning in the early years relies on developing skills in the techniques of observing and assessing these unique individuals with their diverse needs and making use of what you find out. This book provides practical solutions in how to assess and how to plan to ensure that these processes start with the children, keep the children as the central focus, and end with the best support for their individual learning and development. For some practitioners this may mean a big change from what they have done before, whilst for others the book can provide an ideal opportunity to reflect on what they already do, discuss this with the staff team and re-assess strengths.

In all settings, managers, headteachers and practitioners may feel pressure of accountability, both to parents and through the inspection processes. As the EYFS is statutory across the age range, many may feel that it brings more pressure, as every setting – including home-based childminders – is expected to address all aspects of the EYFS relevant to the particular age group they work with. Meeting these demands may seem daunting, but they build on what is already in existence. Most of all, our real accountability is to the children: we owe it to *all* the children to get the planning right. The book stresses how observing children learning and using the information gathered from this for planning 'what next?' can be one of the most rewarding and interesting aspects of the job. Rather than a chore, this can become a delight!

Reflecting on your practice

There are now lots of exciting, innovative child-centred approaches to assessment and planning across the early years sector in all types of settings, which are making a big difference to children. Such practice is not yet universal, and there is always plenty of room for development, whatever your starting point. Reflecting on what you do, how you do it and your areas for development is a vital aspect of good practice. Every setting will have some particular strengths as well as some areas for development – even those settings which

Ofsted has graded as outstanding! Self-evaluation is one of the most important ingredients of the inspection process – a welcome change from the 'done *to*' type of inspection of former years. In order to support the self-evaluation process, each chapter ends with some questions to support the reader's reflection on her/his own strengths and areas for development, and those of the setting.

How this book works

Chapter 1: Starting with the child: policies, principles and processes. This chapter sets the scene by looking at the implications of early childhood policies across the UK, the principles underpinning the EYFS and their likely impact on practice.

Chapter 2: From development matters to effective practice. We turn to consider what we know about child development and what research is telling us about effective practice, from birth to six. There are important implications about how adults can make a real difference to children's learning.

Chapter 3: Planning for every child's learning. This chapter looks at how effective planning depends on information gathered from assessments made from practitioner's observations carried out in the setting. This is called here the 'planning cycle'. The chapter reviews the principles underpinning this cycle.

Chapter 4: Assessment processes across the age range. This chapter shows what to observe across the age range and how best to do it, using a mix of methods to cover a breadth of learning and development, with many real examples. It stresses that a few good-quality observations are far better than lots of observations which give little evidence about what is significant!

Chapter 5: Involving parents, involving children. This chapter considers how best to involve parents and the children themselves fully in observation, assessment and planning processes, with many examples of effective and innovative ways of doing it.

Chapter 6: Linking assessment to planning. Chapter 6 considers the *practicalities* of linking what you have found out from your observations, as well as information from parents and others, to your short-term and medium-term planning.

Chapter 7: Effective practice in action: some case studies. In this chapter there are 'case studies' of practitioners and settings with children across the age range and different types of provision, including a childminder, children's centres, private nursery and schools. They have all developed their own ways of implementing the principles outlined in Chapter 3.

Chapter 8: Supporting transitions and tracking progress. This chapter addresses continuity from one setting to the next, ensuring all aspects of children's wellbeing and development are considered. The practicalities of tracking progress across the EYFS phase and into Year 1 are discussed.

Chapter 9: Managing the processes to support every child's learning. Organisational issues are the topic of this chapter – managing the environment, routines and time to ensure you can plan for all the 'unique' children in your setting. There are suggestions for ways to develop and continually review practice.

Chapter 10: Reflecting back and looking forward. The final word, including the voice of a four year old.

Glossary

Certain acronyms and terminology are used throughout this book which some readers may be less familiar with. The acronyms used are to save space – for example, the early years 'areas of learning' (see below) have very lengthy titles!

- **DfES** – Department for Education and Skills (now the Department for Children, Schools and Families).
- **EYFS** – the English early years framework, the **Early Years Foundation Stage**.
- **Ofsted** is the inspection body inspecting all schools and early years settings in England and Wales.
- **Parents** – used here to include parents, guardians or children's principal carers.
- **Reception class or year** is the final year in the EYFS – various names exist for this year, but we have called it Reception here.

In England, the EYFS has six *areas of learning*.

They are often referred to in the text with the following acronyms:

Personal, Social and Emotional Development (*PSED*)

Communication, Language and Literacy (*CLL*)

Problem-Solving, Reasoning and Numeracy (*PSRN*)

Knowledge and Understanding of the World (*KUW*)

Physical Development (*PD*)

Creative Development (*CD*)

The **EYFS Profile** (replacing the Foundation Stage Profile from September 2008) has thirteen scales, referred to with the following acronyms:

Personal, Social and Emotional Development *(PSED)*

- Dispositions & attitudes *(DA)*
- Social development *(SD)*
- Emotional development *(ED)*

Communication, Language and Literacy *(CLL)*

- Language for communication & thinking *(LCT)*
- Linking sounds & letters *(LSL)*
- Reading *(R)*
- Writing *(W)*

Problem-Solving, Reasoning and Numeracy *(PSRN)*

- Number as labels & for counting *(NLC)*
- Calculating *(C)*
- Shape, space & measures *(SSM)*

Knowledge and Understanding of the World *(KUW)*

Physical Development *(PD)*

Creative Development *(CD)*

Starting with the child: policies, principles and processes

Starting with the child

Every child is different – a unique individual – as any parent with more than one child in their family will know! Each child brings with her or him a very individual wealth of life experiences, relationships, knowledge, understanding and skills. This is true even for a baby of a few months. For older children and adults, we may describe their approach to new experiences as their 'learning style'. With babies and very young children, it is more likely to be described as their responses to experiences and people. Here are some examples.

Finn and **Luna Elis** are almost exactly the same age, they do not know each other, and from just a few months old their different personalities, styles of learning and being, and life experiences have meant that they respond to many new experiences in different ways. They are both two years old.

Luna Elis's mother is Brazilian and she speaks to her in Portuguese; her father is from Spain and he speaks to her in Spanish. She has been brought up from birth in a trilingual environment, with English as the third language she encounters through her parents' English-speaking friends and by living in England. She spends the majority of her time at the age of two with her parents at home or visiting friends, local facilities for young children and two parent and toddler groups. Forming close relationships with others is most important to her – she is shy at first when meeting new adults, many of whom speak to her only in English (the language she is least familiar with). In any new situation where there are other adults and children, she takes it all in slowly. Her parents told me: '*At the groups we go to, it takes her a while to want to socialise – she needs to look around and take it all in first, then gradually she unfolds herself and joins in. She has been going with us for a few months now, and she is getting more confident.*'

Finn approaches everything at a running pace. His parents speak English at home, so this is his only language at this stage. His mother told me: '*His favourite games are chasing games and hide and seek, bouncing, jumping and pretending to be a lion.*' He is confident when meeting new people, focusing at first more on his surroundings than the people. He now goes to a nursery two days a week and has been looked after by his grandmother and grandfather quite often since he was very young. There is a large extended family around him and he has a baby sister of a few weeks' old.

These two children do have a lot in common. They both love being outside and going to local parks. They both love the slides and the swings, role play, getting themselves dressed without help and helping around the house such as with the cooking. They both love balloons, balls and bubbles, exploring the properties of water and paint, getting absorbed in investigating how things work. Yet their approaches to new experiences and new people are very different. It is imperative that they are not treated in the same way if their learning and development is to be supported. As some of their interests are shared, we might want to present them with similar experiences, but unless their concerns and approaches are taken on board, they will not be enabled to participate fully.

Starting right, from the beginning

Practitioners working in the early years need to plan for the children in ways which will build on their responses and approaches to new experiences, their previous experiences and what motivates them. This means finding out about them from their parents and observing them in action. The examples of Finn and Luna Elis show us we need to begin with what we know about them as people, not make vague assumptions about what might seem appropriate for children of this age. This means approaching them differently, planning experiences which build on their interests and what they can already do as well as addressing their anxieties and meeting their needs. This is at the heart of high-quality provision across the age range. It means planning for children's holistic learning and development, supporting them to expand their capabilities, and enabling them to become resilient, emotionally strong human beings. As stated on the EYFS *Principles into Practice* card 1.2:

All children are entitled to enjoy a full life in conditions which will help them take part in society and develop as an individual, with their own cultural and spiritual beliefs.

The update report from the EPPE (Effective Provision of Pre-school Education) research, (Sylva et al, 2007)) notes how *high-quality* early years provision, taking all other factors such as social background into account, continues to have a positive impact on outcomes for children at ten years old. Therefore, provision for young children's development and learning must be of the highest quality if it is to make a positive difference to their lives. Working with young children places a big responsibility on the shoulders of practitioners. This research has continued to track the same cohort of children from age three, and will continue until they are fourteen years old: it has already had a considerable impact on government policy, as was evident in the ten-year strategy document *Choice for Parents, the Best Start for Children* (2004).

Let us now look at some of the policies, principles and processes underpinning early childhood services across the UK.

Policies and principles

A focus on the individual in the early years

In all settings, planning must put children's welfare, development and learning needs first. Throughout the UK there are far-reaching developments to ensure services for all young children become more child-centred and child-friendly. What we know from research about effective practice and child development is taken increasingly seriously in national policy. The statutory and guidance documents across all parts of the UK are underpinned by the view that the provision should revolve around the *children* in order to meet their needs. In Scotland, the '3 Rs'of *Birth to Three: Supporting Our Youngest Children* (2005) – Responsive Care, Relationships and Respect – demonstrate this philosophy clearly. And in England, the Early Years Foundation Stage is organised around four themes: *The Unique Child*, *Positive Relationships* and *Enabling Environments*, as well as *Learning and Development*.

And a focus on the individual for older children too

The approach advocated in the early years is moving up into the primary and secondary sectors. There are developments afoot right through the curriculum in Scotland and an emphasis on 'personalised learning' in England, as highlighted in a policy document referring to 5–19 year olds, looking at the future of education until 2020: '*All schools should reflect a commitment to personalising learning and teaching in their policies and plans . . .*' (DfES, 2006c).

In England too, since 2004, all children's services are aligned under *Every Child Matters*, with its five outcomes of '*stay safe, be healthy, enjoy and achieve, make a positive contribution and achieve economic wellbeing*'.

Early Years across the UK

England: the birth of the EYFS

The Foundation Stage for three to fives, introduced in 2000, reflected and promoted a vision of early education over which there has been a high degree of consensus by early years practitioners for many years. The policy document *Choice for Parents, the Best Start for Children* (2004) set the direction for the most recent developments in early childhood services. This was the birth of the EYFS in England, bringing together the Foundation Stage with *Birth to Three Matters* and many of the *National Care Standards*.

A principled approach

The most significant feature of the EYFS is that it, like its forerunners, is led by a set of clearly defined principles and commitments which all practitioners are expected to embrace. The principles indicate clearly how far we have moved towards the vision so clearly expressed by Loris Malaguzzi, father of the early childhood philosophy in Reggio Emilia in 1993: '*. . . our image of the child is rich in potential, strong, powerful, competent and, most of all, connected to adults and other children.*'

These principles thread throughout every layer of official guidance and additional support materials. They cover all aspects of children's well-being and development under the four interlinked themes mentioned earlier in this chapter. Integral to all the themes is the uniqueness of each child as an individual, the importance of emotional well-being, inclusive practice and children's entitlements, respect for diversity and enabling relationships. For example, the principal statement within the EYFS theme of Learning and Development is:

6 *Children develop and learn in different ways and at different rates and all areas of learning and development are connected to one another and equally important.* 9

One of the biggest changes for practitioners working with children up to the age of three has been that learning and development are organised under the six areas of learning from the Foundation Stage, with their 30 subsections or aspects. Although there were anxieties at the beginning that this might not be appropriate for the very youngest, most agree that they encompass a holistic view of child development. The Early Learning Goals remain as before and almost every 'stepping stone' is incorporated into the 'Development Matters' section of the EYFS.

Wales: the Foundation Phase

In Wales, the early childhood strategy, particularly in relation to pedagogy, continues up to the age of seven. The promise to incorporate five to seven year olds in the Foundation Phase received *'overwhelming support from practitioners and parents alike'* (Welsh Assembly website, FAQs). Starting with a pilot for implementation in schools and settings across Wales in 2006, a clear timeline has been set for the gradual introduction to become the universal curriculum for three to seven year olds by 2011. The curriculum and guidance will start with a clear set of principles and expectations, including the role of play, use of outdoor areas and practitioners making assessments on the basis of their observations. In 2006 the Welsh Assembly issued new guidance for those working with under-threes, entitled *A Flying Start* to *'provide a continuum for children birth to seven.'*

Scotland

In Scotland, a review of the curriculum 3–19 in 2006 proposed radical changes for children from Primary 1 (P1) upwards, but the already well established practice in the early years will continue to build *'on the real strengths: the existing guidance for the curriculum three to five is working well'* (Scottish Office, 2006). There is greater emphasis on continuity between early years and P1, *'more emphasis on active learning through P1 and beyond'* and greater use of observation-based assessment in P1. As mentioned earlier, the guidance for birth to three year olds is organised under the '3 Rs': *Relationships, Responsive Care* and *Respect.*

Northern Ireland

In Northern Ireland a similar review of early years has taken place through the Early Years Enriched Curriculum Evaluation Project, building on findings from EPPNI (Effective Provision of Pre-school Provision, Northern Ireland, Melhuish et al, 2006). Significant changes are planned in relation to the pedagogy and learning experiences encountered by school children in the 4–6 years age range.

The processes: observing, assessing and planning

Most of us who work with young children have chosen to do so because we enjoy it and find it very rewarding. It is the children's excitement and curiosity about the world, their drive to find out about it and the rapidity of development and change at this age which keeps us going. The planning, assessing and keeping of records – all the written work – may seem like an unnecessary chore to do once the children have gone home. Yet it doesn't have to be like this! Observing it is part of the joy, and the discussion between staff in the process of planning from the observations allows you the necessary time to reflect, develop thinking and see the differences you are making to the children.

What are the expectations and requirements for planning and assessment?

The Foundation Stage Curriculum Guidance (DfES, 2000) stated that *'practitioners must be able to observe children and respond appropriately'*. In the EYFS in England, this expectation continues as before, but is now an expectation across the full age range, birth to five, and permeates every aspect, from the Statutory Framework onwards. The EYFS lays *'a secure foundation for future learning through learning and development that is planned around the individual needs and interests of the child, and informed by the use of ongoing observational assessment'* (Statutory Framework, p. 7).

All practitioners are expected to:

❝ Observe children to find out about their needs, what they are interested in and what they can do; note children's responses in different situations; analyse your observations and highlight children's achievements or their need for further support; involve parents as part of the ongoing observation and assessment process. ❞ (EYFS commitment card 3.1)

There is an expectation that practitioners will chart each child's progress and development, based on their observations, in every area of learning, and that there should be open records of the children's learning and development which are regularly shared with parents.

What is expected in terms of planning has changed and developed over the years, with an increased focus on the *intended learning*, rather than a list of activities. This has freed up practitioners to view any specific activity as one of many possible ways to support learning. The important thing is to choose the right one for the child.

Increasingly, the use of new technology is helping with the recording of observations through, for example, the use of digital and video cameras. Planning is increasingly done on the computer – often in the room with the children's help. Many nevertheless prefer handwritten planning to using a computer, as the plans are immediately more accessible to staff and parents, and become more easily flexible. Whatever process is used, the time to analyse what was observed, and to think about what to plan next, continues to be as valuable as ever.

The challenges of planning and assessment in the early years

The principles and requirements emphasise the importance of planning to meet all children's learning and developmental needs. In the case studies (Chapter 7) as well as all the examples from children's records which are used in this book, these practitioners have managed to make the link between their written assessments and planning. However, some find it very difficult, even though they may be very good at doing this in an informal, immediate way.

One of the difficulties often voiced is that an expectation from managers that written plans will be created far in advance make it difficult to respond to children's specific needs. Sometimes, however, it is tradition (*'we have always done it like this'*) which gets in the way. Yet, as the EYFS (3.1, in depth) states:

 ❝ *It is important to remember that no plan written weeks in advance can include a group's interest in a spider's web on a frosty morning or a particular child's interest in transporting small objects in a favourite blue bucket, yet it is these interests which may lead to some powerful learning. Plans should therefore be flexible enough to adapt to circumstances.* ❞

Clear procedures about how to link assessment to planning which are understood by every member of the team, as set out in the following chapters, will help.

Another challenge is how children's records are kept. There is still a tendency in some settings to keep children's records in folders or files shut away in the cupboard or filing cabinet, making it difficult to access them easily or to plan on the basis of the information they contain. Sometimes beautiful, carefully written records have been kept with attractively mounted samples of the children's work, but these are not used for planning and barely referred to when writing an end-of-year summary for parents or the next setting. Inaccessible records mean that planning is much more likely to depend only on what staff have felt is appropriate. Crucially, it also means that the records are not regularly shared with the children and parents.

The best way to understand the planning process is through seeing the processes of observing, assessing and planning as a continuous cycle, as shown in the diagram in Chapter 3. A systematic process is needed which all members of the staff team are aware of, linking what has been collected and recorded about the children with planning. This is the process which the following chapters outline. *'Planning helps me to organise my thoughts and helps me to pick up on what the children like doing and take this forward. Sometimes, though, we might plan to do one thing in a particular way, but it goes in another direction'* (a nursery teacher).

Benjamin is 4 years old. At home with his mother, he has been looking at a favourite new book, *The Story of Everything*, by Neil Layton. The book includes a joke about what the moon is made of. This has caused much curiosity and more jokes about what the moon is made of, playing with words as well as concepts. One discussion which ensued, as Benjamin is half-American, was about the differences in vocabulary – between 'rubbish' (the book is from the UK) and 'garbage'; another involved making a connection between other things he had picked up about the moon: *'Is the moon really made of cheese?'* Later, he rehearses his new understandings – *'some people think it's made of garbage, but it's made of rocks'* – and, taking a walk along the beach near his home, his mother had said *'look, it's high tide'* and his response was *'that's because the moon is pulling in the water'*.

The important question is: what might one do next with Benjamin, to deepen and expand his knowledge and understanding? What support might be given to develop his playful imagination as well as his factual understanding and his interest in two different forms of English?

Observing and listening to children and trying to understand their thinking is a fascinating business for parents and practitioners alike, but not all four year olds will articulate their thinking aloud like Benjamin. As Vivian Gussin Paley (1990) – perhaps one of the best observers of children in our time – put it: *'Whenever I think about children's differences, my sense of the excitement of teaching mounts. Without the uniqueness of each child, teaching would be a dull, repetitive exercise.'* Her inspirational books about young children in her kindergarten class in the USA tell us so much about the role of observation in the process of teaching in the early years.

Using the knowledge you have gained from your analysis of your observations to plan ensures that what you provide is relevant to the children. In fact, it is when planning is fine-tuned to the children that it really becomes rewarding and interesting, and thus enjoyable. If planning was only a question of taking some predetermined learning intentions, and then presenting some predetermined activities for the children to carry out, it would be drudgery indeed!

Here is another four year old, expressing in a different way, through drawing and writing, his interest in making up his own stories. In

Fig. 1.1 *Jason's drawing of his family in a pirate ship (with shark in water below!)*

the drawing he has put his family in the pirate ship: *'They don't know about the shark!'* he said. He then wrote the story himself.

This chapter has outlined some recent developments in the early years policies in the UK. Changes to guidance and requirements are bound to continue as we refine our understanding of child development and effective practice. But whatever changes occur with regard to requirements, goals or curriculum, these will not affect the need for good child-centred planning to ensure every child's learning is supported.

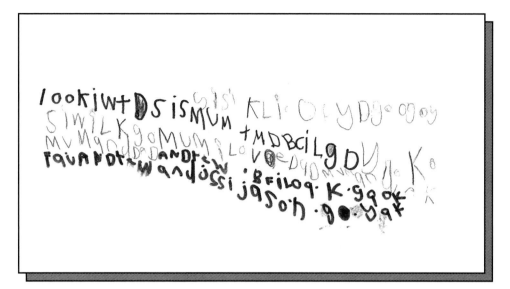

Fig. 1.2 Jason's story ('In my story I am telling my Mum, Dad and sister to look out for the shark.')

Points for reflection

- What works best in your setting to ensure every child is valued and catered for as a unique individual with her/his own approach to new experiences?
- How do you keep records of the children's learning and development? Are these easily accessible, so that they can be used for planning and easily shared?

From development matters to effective practice

2

The EYFS framework is aimed at ensuring the very best for all children. Principles thread throughout all the layers of the framework, guiding the requirements and expectations. The principles come both from what we know about how children learn and from research such as the EPPE research mentioned in Chapter 1 on what makes provision for learning effective. These two strands are clearly visible throughout all four themes in the EYFS: *unique child, positive relationships, enabling environments* and *learning and development.* Provision will not be high quality unless it builds on what we know about how children learn.

What do we know about child development?

Research is constantly refining our understanding and beliefs about child development. Social-constructivism has been the main influence on our understanding of child development in recent years. Children are not only active constructors of their own learning and development, but their learning takes place in and is driven by a social and cultural context in which the child is a key player. As Bertram and Pascal (2006) put it: *'Children are born full of capability, able to communicate, influence and make sense of the world and their experience within it.'*

Empowering relationships and interaction

Babies and young children are totally social beings. They are reliant on others not only for their immediate basic care needs but for stimulation and responsive interaction. They are what Bruner (1981) refers to as *socio-centric*, active and responsive partners in their relationships. Initially of course this is with principal care-givers, but as they grow they begin to relate to other adults and peers. Close emotional ties remain very important: without these, inquisitiveness about the world around will not flourish. *'Children need the chance to experience and benefit from concentrated attention and shared experience from their key person. Otherwise children come to believe that child to adult relationships are only about snatched moments of attention'* (DfES, 2006b).

The zone of proximal development

Vygotsky (1978) emphasised the key role of social interaction in supporting children's learning. Learning takes place when the child is in what Vygotsky called the *zone of proximal development,* described by Wood (1998) as *'the gap between what the child is able to do alone and what he can achieve with help from one more knowledgeable and skilled than himself.'* With the right sort of help and support, the child is ready to take a tiny step in development or even a leap forward. Here is an example.

> **Finn** at 2 years 3 months loves to be outside. At his grandparents' house a new patio is being built. An area has been excavated for the foundations, with planks across a shallow trench which he is very keen to try out for himself. He climbs on and begins to move along. The adult nearby says *'Concentrate, Finn'*. He repeats the word – a new word to him – *'concentrate, concentrate'*, as he negotiates his way along the plank. As he gets to the end he begins to realise that in order to go further he will need to cross a gap onto the next plank which seems too big to manage alone. He looks to the adult for help – just the right amount of physical reassurance, the adult's steadying arm to hold on to if he needs it. Having managed it this way once, he goes around the planks time and time again – each time with more confidence than before. The adult's support remains, just in case.

Brain development

Research on the development of the brain in babies and young children has led to better understanding, for example of the relationship between genetics (biologically determined inheritance) and experience. The brain develops through making connections, or developing 'new wiring', as a result of social relationships, interaction with others and with physical surroundings. From a very early age those connections (synapses) which are reinforced remain and develop, those which are not are pruned. *'What is evident from neuroscience is that "normal" brain development in early childhood is dependent upon environmental input and, for parents and carers, this means warm and loving relationships, appropriate interaction with children in a safe context in which they are nourished and nurtured and allowed opportunities to explore'* (*Birth to Three Matters*, Literature Review, 2003).

Play, active learning and exploration

Children are born with an innate exploratory drive, a motivational impulse to investigate anything and everything.

> **Samual** (2 years 5 months) confidently explored the water feature on the nursery's outing to the Science Museum. He was very focused and interested. He was able to turn the wheel to make the water shoot out, squeeze the large levers and, by experimenting, he learnt that squeezing hard made the water shoot out faster.

Play also affects the development of synapses in all the regions of the brain. It gives opportunities for self-expression and creativity, opportunities to collaborate and negotiate with others, to rehearse and practise newly acquired skills. It enables children to take risks, challenge themselves, imagine, solve problems and create new problems to solve. Play is central to all aspects of learning from birth onwards: social, emotional, cognitive, linguistic and physical. Vygotsky (1978) believed that in play children operate at their highest level, *'beyond his average age, above his daily behaviour; in play it is as though he were a head taller than himself.'*

Schemas

Schemas refer to the 'basic mental framework' which structures early learning (Gura, 1996) or 'threads of action and thought' (Nutbrown, 1994). As Gura puts it: *'Learning develops as a result of attempting to match patterns from the world outside to the schemas in our heads.'*

In some children we see their schematic concerns in everything they do in a much more obvious way than others. We need to know about and record these interests and schemas, whatever form they take, for the children we work with, in order to plan and 'feed' their schemas.

George and **Molly** are twins. At 22 months George showed very clear signs of two schemas in almost everything he did: enveloping and rotation. His childminder, Janet, collected photographic samples for his mother: climbing into cardboard boxes, sitting under a chair (for enveloping) and watching the washing machine, spinning a toy car around (for rotation). Molly, on the other hand, showed no particular dominant schemas at this point. However, at 2 years and 5 months she now has a very obvious lining-up schema, whereas his are now less clear.

Creativity

Creativity is central to being human. As Duffy (1998) puts it, creativity means *'connecting the previously unconnected in ways that are new and meaningful to the individual concerned'*. It is closely linked with imagination, the basis for developing thinking skills, connected to first-hand experiences and memory. Bruce (2004) talks about creativity as a process of incubating and hatching thoughts and ideas: *'Creativity is a complex part of development and learning.'* It can be encouraged to flourish, or it can be stifled – and there are many concerns and research to show that as children grow older, their creativity in school in the UK is all too easily stifled. A misunderstanding of the role of creativity in learning and development has meant that there are often too few opportunities for creativity to blossom in the early years too.

Learning to talk and talking to learn

Gordon Wells (1986) used this phrase 'learning to talk and talking to learn' to encapsulate the role of communication and language in learning. It is through interactions from birth that children begin to develop language skills, and research shows that children are already attuned to their mother's voice in the uterus. Children are not only active partners in the communication – but in most instances the communication *is initiated by* the infant and responded to by the caregiver. It is when a communicative signal from the infant is responded to that learning to communicate is at its most productive. Equally important is 'talking to learn' – learning through language and communication. Language is inextricably intertwined with the development of thinking skills.

> At home **Benjamin**'s mother has been reading him the story *The Tiger who Came to Tea*, by Judith Kerr. Afterwards, Benjamin (4 years 4 months) said, *'Please can you buy me "the lion who came for dinner" and "the jaguar who came for breakfast" and "the monkey who came to play".'*

The nature of intelligence

New ways of seeing intelligence are beginning to influence our understanding about children and learning. For instance, Howard Gardner's (1999) work on the concept of multiple intelligence shows that *intelligence* is not just straightforward intellectual competence, but is composed of at least seven intelligences in different fields: interpersonal and intra-personal, spatial, musical, social, linguistic, and logical. This concept finds synergy with the work of Loris Malaguzzi (1993) in Reggio Emilia, who described children's learning as having 'a hundred languages':

> *The child has*
> *a hundred languages*
> *a hundred hands*
> *a hundred thoughts*
> *a hundred ways of thinking*
> *of playing, of speaking . . .*

Emotional intelligence and emotional well-being

The work of Daniel Goleman (1996) highlights the importance of *emotional intelligence* – having the necessary emotional strength and resilience to cope with life's stresses and strains. Making and maintaining meaningful relationships, coping with one's own and others feelings, developing confidence and independence are all aspects of emotional intelligence. Goleman showed that success in school is more closely linked to emotional factors such as being self-assured and knowing how to behave than to actual IQ. Emotional well-being is a key component of both *Birth to Three Matters* and the EYFS and is increasingly seen as a vital aspect of development and learning throughout the education system (see for example the SEAL materials: DfES, 2004).

In Belgium, Ferre Laevers and his team have been researching the nature of learning in young children for many years. His work on emotional well-being is increasingly used in Britain. He describes well-being as *'feeling like "a fish in water", having vitality, the ability to relax and have fun, and in so doing developing self-confidence and self-esteem'*. He has devised easily identifiable signals for practitioners to assess children's well-being and to focus attention on those children that need the most support by adjusting provision to suit the child.

The concept of involvement

Laevers believes that when children are deeply involved in what they are doing, significant, deep-level learning is taking place. Involvement is related to children's innate 'exploratory drive, motivation and dispositions'. This is how Laevers (2002) describes the concept of involvement: *'When children are concentrated and focused, interested, motivated, fascinated, mentally active, fully experiencing sensations and meanings, enjoying the satisfaction of the exploratory drive, operating at the very limits of their capabilities, we know that deep-level learning is taking place. If deep-level learning is taking place, a person is operating at the limits of their "zone of proximal development".'*

Implications for practice

All we know about child development has significant implications for practice in early childhood provision. It is deep-level learning in young children which will have a lasting effect, and practitioners can either enhance or impede it. Increasing the levels of well-being and involvement will enhance learning. Both well-being and involvement can be observed in children and Laevers has devised systems of indicators of deep-level learning as well as emotional well-being. His 'Involvement Scales' have become a powerful evaluation tool for early childhood settings and schools. The *Effective Early Learning Programme* (Bertram and Pascal, 2004, 2007), well known to many in Britain and abroad as a way of evaluating quality in early years settings, uses his work.

Children's need to explore and investigate, be creative and imagine, develop curiosity and be physically active goes hand in hand with their need for positive and caring relationships. They need to be given time to play and think in a safe and stimulating environment, supported by personal, trusting relationships between practitioners.

Holistic learning

The EYFS provides a meaningful structure for supporting children's learning. Its six areas of learning and development cover the broad spectrum of child development. It reinforces and strengthens the messages from *Birth to Three Matters* and the *Curriculum Guidance for the Foundation Stage* about the holistic nature of learning and development, pointing out that different aspects of development progress at different rates at different times. There are very broad developmental patterns, but given the variations in biological growth and personal experience, each child is unique. The overlapping age ranges cited in the EYFS help to demonstrate this point.

Adults can enhance or extend children's learning, but we can also inadvertently put undue pressure on them, reducing their motivation and confidence. Too often, young children are asked to colour in an *adult's* idea of a house or animal, when their mark-making should be exploratory and free-flowing. Here are typical examples of mark-making by Finn and Luna Elis, the two children aged 2 described in Chapter 1.

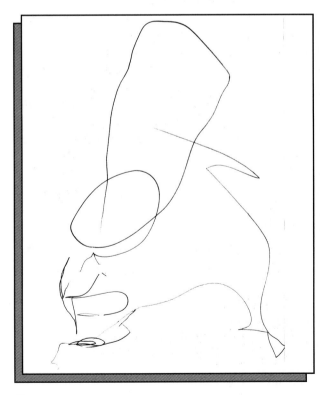

Finn

Luna Elis

Research on effective provision for learning

The Effective Provision of Pre-school Education (EPPE) research has already been mentioned. This longitudinal research project, commissioned by the DfES, has produced some highly significant evidence about what types of early years settings are most effective. The findings for the early-childhood part of the project also had implications for two year olds: *'An early start at pre-school (between 2–3 years) was also linked with better intellectual attainment and being more sociable with other children. The benefits of an early start continue to be evident at the end of Key Stage 1'* (Sylva et al, 2004).

An offshoot from the main project, entitled *Researching Effective Pedagogy in the Early Years* (REPEY), examined the types of 'pedagogy' used in the settings which achieved the highest levels of attainment for children in the EPPE project. Siraj-Blatchford et al (2002) defined pedagogy as not only how adults support learning through their interactions with the children, but also the *context* provided by the adults – the instructive learning environments, routines of the day and relationships with families. Their findings show that good outcomes for children were, amongst other things, linked to practitioners with good curriculum knowledge and knowledge of child development and a strong relationship between parents and practitioners focused on supporting the child's development. The researchers noted a highly significant link between formative assessment (see page 37) and effective pedagogy and giving formative feedback to children during any learning experience. They also noted: *'. . . in the excellent and good settings, the balance of who initiated the activities, staff or child, was very equal, revealing that the pedagogy of these effective settings encourages children to initiate activities as often as the staff.'*

This research is so significant that the EYFS Statutory Framework (p. 11) turns this into a requirement:

> ❦ *All areas [of learning and development] must be delivered through planned purposeful play, with a balance of adult-led and child-initiated activities.* ❦

It goes without saying that if children learn equally from both, then both must be included in what practitioners observe and assess.

Sustained shared thinking

The findings from REPEY also noted that best outcomes for children were linked to *'adult-child interactions that involve "sustained shared thinking" and open-ended questioning to extend children's thinking'*.

'Sustained shared thinking' is the term which the research uses for the best-quality interactions which are likely to lead to learning, where *'each party engages with the understanding of the other'*. To support learning, there needs to be an element of intellectual challenge which is likely to extend thinking. It has to be based in a good level of awareness about the child's interests and understanding, hence the clear link to formative assessment, especially observations. The research also shows that it happens most when the practitioner extends interactions which the child has initiated: *'Freely chosen play activities often provided the best opportunities for adults to extend children's thinking'*.

Supporting social and emotional development

All EYFS practitioners across the age range must ensure that children's need for close relationships, emotional well-being and social interaction are prioritised. This is important for brain development as well as development of a confident well-adjusted child and, later, adult. The younger the child, the more significant the one-to-one relationship between adult and child, and the more vulnerable and reliant on adults the child is in every way. This is the main reason for the child:adult ratios stipulated in the care requirements of the EYFS and the requirement that every child will have an assigned 'key person'.

Supporting children's language development

Wells (1986) compares the way adults support young children in their language development to playing ball with them. The adult has to run to catch the ball when the child throws, but must throw direct into the child's cupped arms for the game to be successful. This type of responsive, conversational support needs to continue well beyond the end of the EYFS, as much recent research on the paucity of the speaking and listening environment in schools shows. This is the kind of 'scaffolding' adults need to give children in *all* their learning. It needs to be at just the right level: not doing things for the children, or leaving them floundering, but supporting them just enough.

Often adults naturally give a running commentary on what is happening when involved in play or any activity with a baby, young child or child new to English. This useful strategy, often used intuitively, models the words and structure of the language for the child within a truly meaningful context. Although the adult is the more experienced partner, it is important to allow the child to communicate too in her/his own way, by leaving room for a potential two-way communication process.

The environment can enable or hinder language development. An environment which supports communication and language provides lots to talk about. In a busy nursery or school setting, there is a need to provide quiet, calm and reflective spaces for small numbers of children to interact quietly together, with and without adults. *'The way that a learning space is set out conveys messages about the sort of interactions that are welcomed and encouraged there'* (Jarman, 2006).

Access to learning for all children: valuing home and community

Mohammed, aged 3, and his family had recently arrived in the country. He was finding the whole process of a new place to live and coming to nursery daunting, especially as no child or adult in the nursery, where there were many bilingual children, shared the same language as him. In order to help him settle, the nursery borrowed favourite music CDs from his parents, and his parents brought in photos of his family to keep at the nursery. The nursery made a photo book about him in the nursery for him to take home. His mother asked a local community organisation to translate some of the children's favourite storybooks into the family's language, extending the nursery's collection of bilingual story tapes by recording one or two. As well as helping Mohammed gain access to the learning experiences on offer, it helped to broaden the resources of the nursery.

The staff regularly evaluated their provision to ensure that all children had equal access to the learning opportunities. They monitored how the children used provision inside and out, checking how boys and girls used it, making sure less confident children were able to use it and ensuring bilingual children were supported to join in group play and activities. They also checked, with the help of parents, that the cultures of the children and of the wider community were reflected in the resources.

All children require support to learn, but different kinds of support and different amounts of support will be needed for different children. An important aspect of helping children to access what is available is to make it meaningful by ensuring their home experiences are valued, celebrated and reflected in the learning environment.

Creating a stimulating learning environment

Both the research mentioned above and what we know about child development point to the need for a stimulating environment which engages children's interests and their drive to explore, experience and investigate. It must be appropriate to the age and all-round development of the children, promoting creativity and thinking skills as well as social, emotional, linguistic and physical skills. It needs to be as stimulating outside as inside if it is to promote learning for all. Children need to spend a large part of their day in play and having playful experiences. Practitioners need to be able to support children in their play, getting alongside and working with them; they need to be able to observe and have time for informal conversations. In the pre-schools of Reggio Emilia the learning environment is referred to as 'the third teacher'.

The Reggio Emilia approach

Over the last two or three decades, there has been increasing interest in the innovative early childhood services in the town of Reggio Emilia in northern Italy. Outcomes for the children are exceptional, in terms of their dispositions, confidence, social development, creativity and general cognitive development. An important aspect of the Reggio Emilia approach is the way that children's interests are built on through projects where children's own ideas lead the investigations. Children are listened to and their thoughts are taken seriously – their creativity forms the core of the curriculum. The emphasis is on discussion, exploration and creative expression. Through documentation which the staff display, the children's thoughts, ideas and creativity are captured.

Louise Boyd Cadwell (1997) believes that underlying the success of the Reggio approach is the way adults perceive children. They are seen as capable, full of potential, curiosity and interest, part of a social network relating to others and part of a community. The practitioner is seen as 'partner, nurturer and guide' as well as researcher. Children and practitioners are given time to think and develop their ideas together. The Reggio ways of working continue to have a profound effect in settings and schools across the UK, influencing pedagogy, assessment processes and planning as well as the way learning is documented and displayed.

Ensuring assessment and planning support the practice

The 'Learning Stories' approach to assessment

Margaret Carr (2001) devised a new approach to early years assessment in New Zealand, based on narrative observations, which she called *Learning Stories*, closely tied to the New Zealand early years curriculum, *Te Whariki*, which focuses attention on developing children's positive dispositions to learning, motivation and social development. *'The stories included the context, they often included the relationship with adults and peers, they highlighted the activity or task at hand . . . and focused on evidence of new or sustained interest, involvement, challenge, communication or responsibility.'*

The assessment process she calls the '4 Ds of assessment': *describing* (what has been observed), *discussing* (with colleagues and others), *documenting* (writing it up, 'recording the assessment in some way') and *deciding* (what to do next). Since her book (and associated training materials) were published, there has been increasing interest and use of this approach to assessment in the UK. Some of the case studies in Chapter 7 used it as their starting point, deeply involving the parents and children.

This chapter has outlined key aspects of child development and recent research on effective support for learning. This must underpin the provision practitioners make for children. But none of it will make sense unless we are able to find out about the children and tailor our support to build on what they can do. Here is a Learning Story which not only shows deep levels of involvement and reflection from two five year olds, but also includes some ideas for 'what next'.

A Learning Story: Building a house or learning to jump?

Fig. 2.1

Fig. 2.2

Evidence:
26/3: **Amy** and **Rojin** were observed in the outdoor area totally involved for about three-quarters of an hour, building what appeared to be an obstacle course. However, asking one of the children later, with the help of the photographs, provided a different picture.

The Child's View

Amy: *'I was playing with Rojin outside together – we tried to look for L'* (a girl who usually plays with them but was not in school that day). *'We were making a house but we wanted L to help. It was Rojin's idea to make the house. We were jumping over but couldn't get to that bit, so we crossed over there.'*

The Practitioner's View

Assessment: *what does this show about the child's learning and development?*

They both kept this going for a long period of time, totally absorbed in their play. In the process of building the house, they were using their awareness of length, shape and space to make a grid pattern. As they did so, they practised their own physical skill development and abilities, challenging themselves to jump the gap. They kept on experimenting, moving the planks into new positions.

Areas of learning: *KUW: designing and making*; *PSED: SD*; *PSED DA*

Implications for planning: *what next?*

Ask the girls how they would like to follow this up: could they develop an obstacle course for others? Find imaginative stories about houses of all sorts, building houses, houses with gaps in the floors . . .

Points for reflection

- Looking at the aspects of child development and research outlined in the first part of this chapter, which aspects are most relevant to you and your setting in further developing understanding of children's learning?
- Looking at the 'implications of effective practice', how do you ensure they are reflected throughout your setting?

Planning for every child's learning

Throughout the EYFS, beginning with the Statutory Framework, the message comes through loud and clear: planning should start from what you know about the children you have now in your setting, whether this is the very youngest or children at the end of the reception year in school. It has become a requirement (p. 20):

❛ *Providers must plan and organise their system to ensure that every child receives an enjoyable and challenging experience that is tailored to meet their individual needs.* ❜

Elsewhere this message is expanded (p. 11):

❛ *All practitioners should . . . look carefully at the children in their care, consider their needs, their interests and their stages of development and use all of the information to help plan . . . across all areas of learning and development.* ❜

In Chapter 1 we began by looking at two children, both of the same age, with some common interests, but much which was different in how they approach things. Planning for them should be very different. As Sandy, the Birth to Three coordinator at Fortune Park, put it: *'We are responsible for providing appropriate space, resources and props based on our knowledge and observations of young children, providing opportunities that will extend their imagination and give their play the quality it deserves. We need to know children as individuals just as they need to know us, they need to feel supported and cared for as we do . . .'*

There are different timescales for planning – the longer term provides the overview, the *background* (which will be discussed at the end of this chapter), but it is short- and medium-term planning which are key to ensuring every child *can* learn and develop.

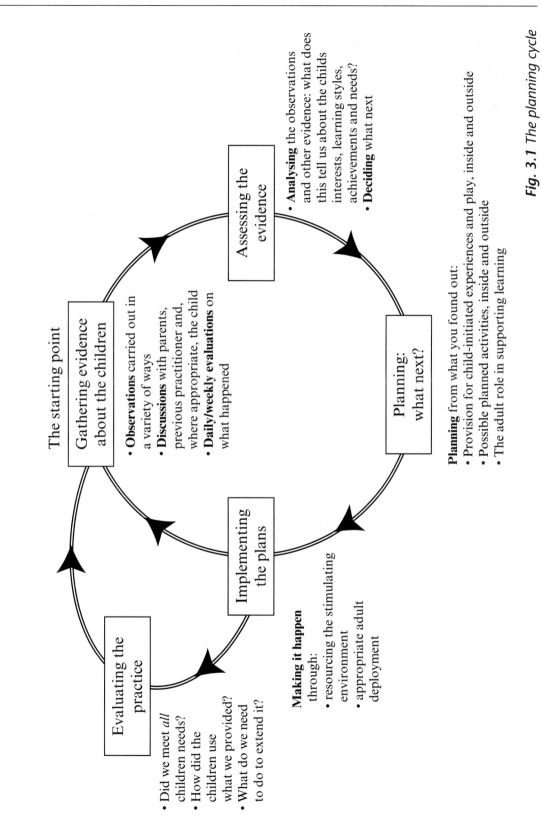

The starting point

Gathering evidence about the children

- **Observations** carried out in a variety of ways
- **Discussions** with parents, previous practitioner and, where appropriate, the child
- **Daily/weekly evaluations** on what happened

Assessing the evidence

- **Analysing** the observations and other evidence: what does this tell us about the childs interests, learning styles, achievements and needs?
- **Deciding** what next

Planning: what next?

Planning from what you found out:
- Provision for child-initiated experiences and play, inside and outside
- Possible planned activities, inside and outside
- The adult role in supporting learning

Implementing the plans

Making it happen through:
- resourcing the stimulating environment
- appropriate adult deployment

Evaluating the practice

- Did we meet *all* children needs?
- How did the children use what we provided?
- What do we need to do to extend it?

Fig. 3.1 The planning cycle

The planning cycle

Planning starts with observing and getting to know the children. It needs to ensure what is provided is fun and helps them to develop – and to do this it must start off from where they are. Figure 3.1 shows how the process works. I call this 'the planning cycle', but planning is the *end* point in the cycle. The cycle starts with 'gathering evidence' and this means observing and finding out about the children (from their parents and those who know them well). From the evidence gathered, a decision is made – this is the assessment process. This in turn feeds the planning, which is then implemented and the cycle continues.

This is the '4 Ds' process Margaret Carr (2001) uses in her work on Learning Stories: *describing, discussing, documenting, deciding*, as described on page 35. When the cycle works effectively, it is a quick and automatic process.

Different types of assessment

There are two types of assessment: formative – assessment *for* learning, which informs planning – and summative assessment – the assessment *of* learning at a point in time. The EYFS Profile is the summative assessment which is a statutory requirement at the end of the Foundation Stage, but it is the ongoing formative assessment, based on and adapting to observations, which helps children to learn. The REPEY research (Siraj-Blatchford et al, 2002), mentioned in Chapter 2, has shown clearly that where formative assessment is effectively used in early years settings, the quality of learning is at its best: *'The research shows that the more knowledge the adult has of the child, the better matched their support and the more effective the subsequent learning.'*

The most important source of knowledge comes from observing the children. Observations are likely to show what motivated the child, who else was involved, why it happened and something about dispositions, as well as skills and understanding. Deciding what any observation tells you is the formative assessment.

Assessment for learning

Formative assessment has increasingly been associated with what is called *assessment for learning*. The processes described in the diagram are akin to the assessment for learning processes promoted widely as a crucial aspect of primary and secondary teaching. The term *assessment for learning* was originated by the Assessment Reform Group and the work of Black and Wiliam, who examined a wide range of research on improving teaching and noted the significant effect on outcomes in studies which involved improving formative assessment practice. They concluded: *'Assessment which is specifically designed to promote learning is the single most powerful tool we have for both raising standards and empowering lifelong learners'* (Assessment Reform Group, 1999).

Starting planning from observation and assessment

In order for the planning cycle to work effectively, practitioners need to understand why the steps in the process are important and how the processes work. In two of my previous books (Hutchin, 1999, 2003) I have emphasised the importance of starting with a set of principles to underpin practice. Many have found this a useful starting point to reviewing their practice. My principles are re-stated and explained here, with implications for practitioners and practice. Many of these are now echoed in the principles of the EYFS.

Principle 1

The starting point for assessment is the child, *NOT* a predetermined list of skills against which a child is marked.

> *Implications: Observing children is the starting point for assessment, **not** a checklist – this means not using the EYFS Development Matters, Early Learning Goals or EYFS Profile scale points in this way!*

Children are all unique individuals and what is a small step for one child is just as significant a leap for another, yet a predetermined list of skills will not show these important personal developments and achievements. Neither will it produce the kind of focused, responsive interaction and support which is necessary to meet children's learning needs.

With the introduction of the Foundation Stage in 2000, it became increasingly common for practitioners to use the Stepping Stones and Early Learning Goals as assessment statements. The Stepping Stones were intended as guidance only, but were often treated as a predetermined list of skills. When *Birth to Three Matters* was published, some educational resource providers devised similar checklists for children under three. This was certainly not the intention of either document: the EYFS has been much more determined and explicit in ensuring this does *not* happen. With reference to the Development Matters sections, the Practice Guidance (p. 11) states, in bold type:

❛ *These sections are not intended to be exhaustive . . .* **they should not be used as checklists.** ❜

Principle 2

Observations and records show what the children *CAN* do – their significant achievements – not what they *can't* do.

> Implications: Are records always written in a positive way? If records only note what the child has achieved, how can they support planning? How can we ensure learning needs are also highlighted without being negative? Are expectations high for every child?

The dangers of negative assessments

Sometimes I see comments in children's records such as *'poor language skills'* or *'can't relate to other children'*. These are not observations, but negative, judgemental statements. Such comments only tell us that the person writing them has dismissed the child as incapable in some way. Other comments, made about children in adult-led activities, such as *'refused to write'* or *'showed no interest'*, just show that the planning for the child was wrong, not that the child was wrong. We have no right to condemn a young child's learning by speaking or writing negative statements. Assessment should *motivate* children to continue. It should boost confidence and self-esteem as well as acknowledging the achievement – however small a step the achievement was. Lancaster (2006) reminds us of the tendency in Western culture for a deficit model of childhood, seeing children only as a person 'in training', thus limiting our views of their capabilities.

An observation describes an action, event or moment in time. As such, it cannot be negative. If an aspect of a child's development is causing concern, then it is crucial to describe in detail what was seen. The judgement comes when *analysing* the observation, focusing on what the child *can* do, as well as what she/he needs help with. A question that frequently arises is: what about when a child's behaviour is unacceptable? If, for example, a conflict has been observed, it is important not to ignore it but to record it, as with any other observation. It is in the analysis that the need for further support should be highlighted. It is important to remember that it is the adult who is in control, not the child.

Evidence:

Danny, a three year old, making Duplo models on carpet with five others. Conflict ensued when he grabbed a piece of Duplo from another child. Conflict resolved when staff member intervened.

Assessment: *What does it tell us about this child's learning and development?*

In a situation where a number of children are working with a limited amount of resources, Danny needs *support* to ask for what he wants and wait his turn.

Implications for planning: *what next?*

* Organise construction provision so that children are encouraged to choose from the range of sets (and possibly limit numbers of children in the area?).

* Ensure a member of staff is deployed here daily for a week, to introduce new system of free choice and to support Danny in asking for what he wants and seeing the possibilities of using alternative resources.

The dangers of low expectations

Do we have a ceiling on our expectations for some children? Unconsciously we often make negative judgements about other people based on a particular feature or characteristic, such as ethnicity, culture, ability, religion or gender. This is called *stereotyping*. Stereotyping is highly damaging to all concerned – the person doing it as well as the recipient of it. We may limit our expectations of certain children because of this, but it also limits us: *'If expectations of children from particular groups are based on negative stereotypes, they could be labelled as non-achievers and therefore not expected to achieve. Thus educators set up a self-fulfilling prophecy – they get the results they expected. The children pick up subtle and overt messages that they are not expected to succeed intellectually and behave accordingly'* (Brown, 1998).

It is crucial to understand and value diversity and keep an open mind. The onus is on the adults involved to ensure the best possible support to the child.

Brown (1998) also helps us to understand that: *'Children can become active, enthusiastic and independent learners, if, as their educators, we value their cultures and communities and understand how racism and other social inequalities influence their lives.'*

Principle 3

Practitioners observe children as part of their daily routine.

> *Implications: How can observation become an integral part of the adult's role in any setting? What skills do practitioners require in order to observe?*

What do we mean by *observing*? The dictionary definition includes the notion not only of *watching* but also *taking note*, with an intention of doing something as a result. There is a strong element of *purposefulness* in this concept. If observing is to be useful, it requires:

■   thorough understanding of child development and *how* children learn;
■   knowledge of a range of observation techniques, so that the most appropriate can be chosen for the occasion at hand;
■   a general idea of what to look for;
■   an ability to keep an open mind, so that the unexpected, which is so often very significant, can be noted;
■   an ability to write meaningful notes quickly;
■   skills in making an assessment from what has been observed.

Observation needs to become a habit, incorporated into daily practice through a systematic process. There is no expectation that observations will go on all the time, or that *everything* that children do has to be observed, but observation should be an integral part of everyday practice. Chapter 4 gives more detailed information and plenty of examples of the processes involved.

Principle 4

Children are observed in play, in self-chosen activities as well as planned adult-directed activities.

> *Implications: Are practitioners looking at children's learning holistically, and valuing what they do, taking note of the full range of situations they engage in across the day?*

The findings of the REPEY research, referred to earlier, demonstrate the need for a balance of child-initiated learning and adult-led activities for best outcomes for children. However, observing a child in play and self-initiated activities is likely to be even more important than in adult-led activities because, as Vygotsky has shown, it is these types of activities where children show their greatest competence. The outcomes from play and self-initiated learning are far less predictable – and therefore much more worthwhile to observe – than adult-directed activities with specific expected outcomes. Every observation of children in play will provide information covering several aspects and areas of learning and development, as the examples in the next chapter will show.

In 2006 the National Assessment Agency stated in relation to the Foundation Stage Profile (forerunner to the EYFS Profile) that 80% of evidence of children's achievement should be gathered from what children do independently, in their own self-chosen activities and play. This is now in the Statutory Framework (p. 16) in relation to the EYFS Profile: *'Judgements against these [Profile] scales . . . should be made from observation of consistent and independent behaviour, predominantly children's self-initiated activities.'* Some of the most significant learning will often take place in unplanned contexts – there are several examples in Chapter 4.

Principle 5

Observations should note the child's interests, passions and concerns as well as how the child is learning.

> *Implications: How can we make use of this information in our assessments and planning?*

Knowing what a child is showing particular interest in – and often passionate about – is vital in planning. This is what motivates a child to develop her/his skills and to explore and experiment. Whatever the age and stage of development of the child, the child's interests will be what she/he is focusing on and thus the most effective medium for learning something new. This means that it is important when analysing observations not just to concentrate on *what* the child may have learnt, but to highlight *how* the learning happened too. The children's interests should become *vehicles* for learning.

George (aged 2) was interested in the cartoon film *Finding Nemo*. The Children's Centre's visit to the London Aquarium, on the basis of this interest, led to an enormous amount of learning for so many of the two year olds involved – in language, concept development, knowledge about fish, transport, journeys, relationships with new people and so on.

Principle 6

Observations are analysed to highlight achievements and needs for further support, and used for planning 'what next?'

> *Implications: How can we link planning and assessment effectively when every child is an individual?*

This is the very heart of assessment for learning and the reason for observing and gathering evidence about each child's learning, as discussed earlier in this chapter and shown in Figure 3.1 (page 33). Chapter 6 outlines the practical processes involved, and Chapter 9 is devoted to supporting manageability of the processes.

Principle 7

Parents' contributions to the assessment process are central.

> *Implications: How strong is the partnership with parents? Are parents involved in contributing their observations as well as participating in more formal discussions about their child?*

Parents need to be the starting point of a child's record, as they will contribute key information about their child's learning and development at home. This then needs to continue throughout the early years and beyond. Chapter 5 looks in detail at ways of involving parents. The involvement of parents is also an important part of the EYFS Profile.

Principle 8

Children must be involved in their own assessment, and their voices heard, regardless of age or ability

> *Implications: Is assessment something which is done **to** or **with** the children in your setting or school?*

Young children start out in life with an innate motivational impulse to explore, learn and make sense of the world. It is the *child* who learns: we cannot learn *for* her/him, although we can certainly help. But if assessment is something we perform *on* children, rather than involve them *in*, then we miss the opportunity for them to be able to become reflective and celebrate their achievements, and we are in danger of taking away their initiative in what *else* needs to be learnt or tackled. We need to ensure that children have a voice in their own assessment and in planning the next steps – even at this young age. Ways of involving children in their own assessment, as well as involving their parents and carers, is the focus of Chapter 5.

Principle 9

All records are open, accessible and shared regularly with parents and the children concerned.

> *Implications: Are your records kept in such a way that they can be easily shared with the children and parents?*

The case studies in Chapter 7 show some good ways of keeping all the observations and records of children open and accessible. The most important thing is, as described in Chapters 1 and 4, to keep every child's record as a personal profile of that child alone, not in a folder with all the others, kept out of sight.

Principle 10

The child's record of achievement should be regularly reviewed and summarised, to ensure the child's progress is tracked and learning and development are appropriately catered for.

> *Implications: When, how often and how should we make summaries of ongoing assessments of children's learning and development within the EYFS?*

The only *required* summative assessment is at the end of the EYFS, before a child moves into Year 1, yet children may move into a setting at any time from birth onwards and most move between settings during the EYFS. Reviews of all the evidence from parents and observations, samples, photographs and other forms of recordings – in fact the whole of a child's record – should be carried out regularly and, when a child leaves, passed on to the next setting. More information on how to manage the process is spelt out in Chapter 8.

Applying the principles

Many settings and childminders have incorporated principles such as these into their practice for a number of years, but this has not been universal. For some, perhaps most commonly in the reception year, planning is still seen as something to be done way in advance. It is important to acknowledge the different timescales of planning: the planning cycle described here and the principles for assessment and planning refer to *short-* and *medium-*term planning, adjusted daily and weekly on the basis of the observations and information from parents and others involved. Providing the *background* to all the provision that every setting and school makes is the *long-*term planning overview.

Planning the overview: long-term planning

Carla Rinaldi (2001) calls planning *'a forecast of possibilities within an arena of opportunities'*. In the short term the 'forecast of possibilities' is for now, tomorrow or during the next few days, suggesting ways forward. But then there is the *overview* of possibilities: what do we want all the children to have developed whilst they are here in this setting? Looking at planning as 'possibilities' helps us to think more broadly, raising our expectations of what might be.

'Long-term planning is concerned with children's entitlement' (Fisher, 1998). It is most important that it is seen in this way: what are the opportunities that should be provided for *all* the children in our care? Is this to be different for different age groups, and are there elements which should be the same regardless of age? It does *not* mean devising a list of themes or topics to run over the year, but focuses on planning the ethos, environment, principles and values. Broadly, the EYFS gives every setting and every practitioner the overall expectations for planning. The principles and commitments

steer the ethos, environment and climate for high-quality care and support for learning. It also gives an overview of what to provide for children's learning and development.

Even though it may appear that the EYFS does the long-term planning for you, it is very important that practitioners in every setting meet together to discuss this 'entitlement' and how to interpret it. As the EYFS (3.1, in depth, p. 6) states:

> *Long-term planning provides a structure which helps you ensure that you cover all the areas of Learning and Development and the Principles in the EYFS.*

It provides the framework to review what you do now. Are the routines organised around the children, so that these respond to their needs rather than adult convenience? Is the learning environment planned to ensure it values, celebrates and responds to the ethnic and cultural diversity of the wider community and wider world? Are you providing a rich emotional, physical and social environment for *all* children to progress in their learning and development?

Although there is broad guidance in the EYFS in relation to planning, and a few examples of planning in different settings, there is no requirement to plan in a particular way – leaving it up to the individual setting and their circumstances. The next few chapters provide more detail on the various aspects of the short- and medium-term planning cycle, beginning with the practicalities of observation and assessment.

Points for reflection

The planning cycle is dependent on effectively implementing the principles outlined in this chapter. Use them to review your own processes: do your assessment and planning processes match with the underpinning principles and ethos of your setting?

1   The starting point for assessment is the child, *NOT* a predetermined list of skills against which a child is marked.

2   Observations and records show what the child *CAN* do – significant achievements – not what she/he *can't* do.

3   Practitioners observe children as part of their daily routine.

4   Children are observed in play and self-chosen activities as well as, where appropriate, planned adult-directed activities.

5   Observations should note the child's interests, passions and concerns, as well as how the child is learning.

6   Observations are analysed to highlight achievements, needs for further support and used for planning 'what next?'

7   Parents' contributions to the assessment process are central.

8   Children must be involved and their voices heard, regardless of age and ability.

9   All records are open, accessible and shared regularly with parents and the children concerned.

10 The child's record of achievement should be regularly reviewed and summarised to ensure her/his progress is tracked and learning and development are appropriately catered for.

Assessment processes across the age range

4

As wide a range of evidence as possible is needed to create a full picture of a child's achievements to ensure the provision and practitioners' responses to the child enable and extend learning. In this chapter we will consider the practicalities of observing and collecting evidence of children's learning and development and how to 'put it to good use' (Drummond, 1993). We need to be aware that: *'A child's response during a single activity is not always an accurate or reliable guide to underlying competence. Therefore there needs to be caution about conclusions drawn on the basis of one activity alone'* (SCAA, 1997).

Observations need to be made over time in different situations and at different times of day to cover the breadth of learning opportunities provided. But the effectiveness of the assessment and planning processes rests not on the *quantity* of observations but on the *quality* and *significance* of the evidence gained.

Not every observation will be written down – that would be impossible! But writing down an observation or taking a digital photograph is both an important memory aid for the practitioner and provides something tangible to analyse and to share with the child, the parents and other staff. The case studies in Chapter 7 provide good evidence of this in action, across the age range. Recent developments in digital technology, such as digital cameras and video, have significantly aided the observation process. They cut out the need for lengthy descriptions of complex play scenarios and have proved so useful for sharing with the children and parents. But they do not substitute for the *assessment*: every piece of evidence still needs to be analysed in some way, drawing out the significant learning and development.

Different types of observations will result in different kinds of evidence. Taken altogether, these will result in rich evidence about learning. Using a mix of observation methods and a variety of situations to observe is the best way of ensuring you have an effective record-keeping and planning process to supporting the children's learning. Practitioners from other agencies will sometimes be involved: it is important to share with them the observation, assessment and planning processes used in your setting.

What are the practical processes involved?

Although the evidence itself may come in very different forms – for example, a photograph, drawing or observation – and the record-keeping format may differ from one setting to another, the process remains the same: from observing to assessing to planning. All the examples in this chapter follow this procedure. The format below provides a practical way of embedding this into day-to-day practice:

> **Evidence (observation or example):**
>
> **Assessment:** *what does this show about the child's learning and development?*
>
> **Area(s) of learning addressed:**
>
> **Implications for planning:** *what next?*

These processes require skills in observing, writing observations, analysing the evidence and making assessments, and finally deciding what to do next as a result of what was seen.

What to observe

For babies and younger children, you should be noticing everything the children interact with, even a concentrated gaze. Most of what you observe and therefore note down or photograph will be things you feel are significant. For older children in a nursery or reception setting, however, it is useful to break down these opportunities the children are provided with into three categories, as this will aid your planning:

- play and child-initiated activities, inside and outside;
- adult-initiated activities inside and outside which, for some of the time, adults participate in and some of the time children do independently;
- adult-led activities, inside and outside.

For any age, the majority of observations need to be of the children in play – in what they have chosen to do. Practitioner-led activities generally give the least useful information as they are much more predictable than what the child chooses to do independently. This was explained in Chapter 3. Look out for particular interests, the child's level of involvement and which aspect grabs the child's attention most. Although you may have an idea of what you are looking for, it is essential to keep an open mind so that you don't miss other valuable developments. The following example illustrates this point:

> Observing a three or four year old child in a small group of children in the home corner, the practitioner might intend to observe how the child relates to others (social development). In the course of the observation she/he may also notice how the child:
>
> - *makes connections between real life experiences and fantasy play – often in unexpected ways;*
> - *shows confidence, enthusiasm and independence (dispositions);*
> - *sequences an event such as cooking;*
> - *dresses and undresses with dressing-up clothes;*
> - *writes a message on the telephone pad in own emergent writing;*
> - *explains to another child how something worked;*
> - *develops the story line for the play in collaboration with another child.*
>
> In the space of a three-minute observation, a great deal of information about the child's all-round development can be gathered (Hutchin, 2006).

How to observe

An observation needs to describe as accurately as possible what was seen and/or heard. The important thing is to write down in short, quick notes just what seems to be significant. This means things you don't already know, anything new, different or just not previously recorded – there is no need to write lengthy details about everything that happens during the observation or things you know already. Noting what the children said through spoken language or their preferred medium is particularly useful. This fulfils two functions: first, it provides a window into how they are thinking and, second, it gives evidence of their use of language. Non-verbal communication and gesture is as important, especially with younger children.

All staff need to get into the habit of noting down things and taking photographs as they work. Different types of activities and experiences provided for children need a different type of observation technique, *depending on the practitioner's role within the activity* – i.e. whether it is adult-led or child-initiated. The different types of observations are likely to be as follows:

Participant observations

- when adult is involved in play with the children;
- when adult is involved in planned practitioner-led activities (mainly with older children).

Incidental observations (catch-as-you-cans)

- when you notice something significant that you are not involved in.

Conversations with children

- informal conversations and discussions which are noted down;
- 'interviewing' children about their own learning and interests (see Chapter 5).

Recordings

- photos of children carrying out a particular activity or involved in play, showing the learning process;
- video;
- audio recordings of play or discussions.

Samples

- drawings, independent emergent writing, photos of models, art work, etc.

Planned, 'focused', narrative observations

- in which the observer deliberately stands back to observe and does not become involved.

Many settings use an *observation diary* format, with blank spaces, to stick their observations written on Post-its or self-adhesive labels. Some write all their observations on pre-prepared slips of paper, with headings similar to those used here.

Making the assessments

Every observation needs to be analysed, to explore what learning is taking place, drawing out what was significant or new. The key questions are:

What does this tell us about this child's learning and development?

What areas or aspects of learning and development are evident?

Following the format used in this chapter will help. Sometimes the analysis may require a few moments' thinking time or a quick discussion at the end of the day or session. For a childminder this will most probably be a discussion with the child's parents. With older children, sharing what you wrote down with the child afterwards can help to boost self-esteem and confidence while also adding significantly to your assessment. Some of the examples in this chapter demonstrate this. The best way of doing this with younger toddlers and babies is through photographs. When observing play, it can be helpful to have some assessment questions to hand (Figure 4.1). There is *no* expectation that practitioners will look for *all* of these!

Implications for planning

Every observation or evidence is likely to have *some* implications for planning for the individual child, and on a broader level for the setting – such as changing a routine or introducing something new. A set of questions to consider when asking *'What next for this child?'* might be:

What can we do to extend this child's skills or understanding in relation to what has been observed?

What activities, learning opportunities or resources should we provide?

How will staff be involved?

For the setting and staff, implications for planning might be:

What do we need to change or develop as a result of what we saw?

How can we encourage other children to join in?

Can all children access the full range of learning opportunities we provide?

The majority of evidence will consist of participant observations, incidental 'catch-as-you-cans' as well as samples and photographs. However, another important type of observation is the planned, 'focused', *narrative* observation. The evidence from this is likely to be of a very different nature, and very worthwhile if the child is involved in something they have chosen to do, capturing significant evidence which otherwise might be missed.

Personal, Social and Emotional Development

Dispositions and attitudes: Who initiated the play/activity? How involved was the child – did she/he show interest, persistence/determination? Did the child introduce new ideas or change the focus? How confident did the child seem? Did the child select or create any 'props' to use – if so, how?

Social development: Was there any new evidence of building relationships, negotiating, sharing and cooperating with others? Was there evidence of respect for others and growing cultural awareness?

Emotional development: How did the child express feelings and/or respond to the feelings of others? Was there evidence of growing control over own behaviour – if so, how was this shown?

Communication, Language and Literacy

What type of language (including non-verbal communication) was in evidence? With the youngest children, look for gestures, sounds, early words; with older children, look for evidence of: talk (in preferred language, including signing) about present, past or future events; sustaining a conversation with adult or child; expressing imaginary or real ideas; using language to create or add to a storyline; questioning or clarifying thoughts. Was there evidence of any developing literacy skills?

Problem-Solving, Reasoning and Numeracy

What evidence was there of problem solving and reasoning with a mathematical focus (e.g. sorting, matching, classifying, comparing, counting, sharing out and calculating)? Was there evidence of any mathematical language?

Knowledge and Understanding of the World

Exploration and investigation: What evidence was there of interest in exploring, observing, investigating, cause and effect, making predictions or giving explanations? Was there talk about how things work and, if so, what?

Physical Development

Was there evidence about the child's developing fine or gross motor skills?

Creative Development

Was there evidence of developing or sustaining a storyline, taking on a role or assigning roles to others, using props creatively? Was there evidence of integrating other creative forms such as dance, music or movement?

Fig. 4.1 Assessing a child in play or child-initiated activities: some useful assessment questions across the age range

Storing the ongoing records

There are lots of ways of storing the records and practitioners need to decide on the best way for their needs. It is worth considering the following points:

- Are they easily accessible to staff and children?
- Can they be easily shared with parents?
- Do they show that you value each child as an individual and show respect for all-round achievements?

The best approach is to create an individual record of achievement, profile book or portfolio for each child: this is a must if records are to be open, accessible and shared. Some practitioners keep their collected samples accessible to the children and parents in a portfolio and the observations elsewhere in a file. Although I think it is much better in terms of accessibility to staff and children if both can be kept together, many of the case study settings (Chapter 7) feel that this would be unwieldy for the youngest children, reducing accessibility. It needs careful thought to decide what is best for your children and your setting, but the important message throughout this book is: all records need to be open, written positively, respecting the child and family, and focused on the child's achievements and how to extend these.

For the acronyms used to identify areas of learning: see page 6.
In these examples you will note how, as stressed in the EYFS, different children develop at different rates.

Planned, focused observations

This is the only type of observation where the practitioner needs to stand back without being involved, to watch and record a narrative observation. Practitioners should aim to do one of these on every child regularly – in nursery and reception classes I recommend once per term: in a toddler room, it may be once every six weeks. It requires full involvement in the job of observing, taking down as much relevant detail as possible. This should not be unmanageable as they are *planned* observations. The time needed to do them is relatively short – 4 to 5 minutes is usually enough.

Organising the observations

In a reception class with 30 children, observing three children per week in this way will mean that in ten weeks the whole class will have been observed. Some teachers prefer to ensure that one is done every day, so that every child can be observed in 6 weeks – perhaps the second half of the autumn term, the middle six weeks in the spring term and early part of the summer term. Others prefer to do three on one day of the week. The same applies with babies and toddlers and, as staffing ratios are greater, the observations can be done more frequently. But remember: they are useful *only if* the child is involved in play or a self-chosen activity. It is the adult's *time to observe* which is planned, not the child's activity!

Although some practitioners feel that this is the type of observation which is the hardest to manage during a busy day, it *is* possible and many practitioners manage with no difficulties. The key to success is to ensure that the children can work and play independently and purposefully without the need to intervene to help children access resources or sort out squabbles. A well-managed learning environment is essential – and as we all know, it does makes a huge difference to children's success in learning. Chapter 9 has more details on managing the process.

I find the best method for this type of observation is a four- or five-minute continuous observation. In planning it, you will need to decide what type of observation you will do, who will be carrying out the observations, when and for how long, and how you will choose which children to observe (e.g. each child in your group in rotation?). Add this information onto the weekly planning sheet, adjusting your plans accordingly to ensure it takes place. It is a valuable aspect of your practice – not an add-on extra!

Making the assessment

Make assessments of the child's skills, knowledge, understanding and attitudes where these show a difference from what staff already know, as outlined above. Include a note on what particular aspect of the activity seems to interest the child most. A useful way to make the assessment is to divide it up under different areas of learning, making a judgement under each *relevant* area of learning. Using an observation format specifically designed for the purpose, as in the examples on pages 64–6, will help you analyse the observation.

Participant observations

These observations are usually written on prepared slips of paper, Post-its or self-adhesive labels, which are then added to the child's record.

Participating in play outside and inside

Evidence: 5/10/06

Rebecca, 1 year 7 months

Matched the pieces of an animal inset puzzle to the picture, by placing the animals on top of the right pictures. Self-corrected a couple of times.

Assessment: *what does this show about the child's learning and development?*

Interested in matching independently with no adult prompting and was able to correct herself

Areas of learning: *PSRN*

Implications for planning: *what next?*

Develop her interest in matching.

Evidence: 27/2/07

Billy; 3 years 11 months

In role play area set up as Chinese restaurant, in the role of waiter: *'They need chapadums'*, holding up two chopsticks. Adult: *'Do you mean chopsticks?'* *'Yeah,'* said Billy, *'Silly me! Chopsticks!'*

Assessment: *what does this show about the child's learning and development?*

Really grasping well at new vocabulary here, although got into a bit of a muddle with the right new words; saw the funny side of it!

Areas of learning: *CLL: LCT; KUW; CD*

Implications for planning: *what next?*

Introduce proper names for familiar Chinese foods and other kitchen/eating tools.

Planned adult-directed activities, inside and outside

Evidence: 11/11

Samual, 2 years 8 months

Joined in the planned cooking activity. Interested in cutting courgettes, initially supported by staff then independently. Sustained this activity for much longer than usual.

Assessment: *what does this show about the child's learning and development?*

This seems a very good choice of activity, to build up his sustained concentration – he was obviously involved at a deep level. May be using tools is the important aspect to sustain interest and build skills? Or is it link with home?

Areas of learning: *PSED: DA; PD*

Implications for planning: *what next?*

Provide tools such as play knives and scissors with other materials such as clay, playdough and more cooking! Ask mum about his involvement in cooking at home.

Evidence: 21/11

Arane, 4 years 1 month

In Tamil (her first language) she tells the bilingual assistant: *'Saturday and Sunday – no school. I didn't come to school yesterday.'*

Assessment: *what does this show about the child's learning and development?*

Concept of time and events developing well, correct names for days of the week as well as sequencing of days.

Areas of learning: *PSED: DA; KUW: sense of time*

Implications for planning: *what next?*

Continue this and also add in smaller and greater units of time to sequence (continue in Tamil at this time, so that concept development is not held up by competency in speaking English).

Participating in large-group planned activities

For older children, usually from the age of three upwards, large-group activities are a part of the normal day – for example, for a shared story or songs and rhymes and for teaching specific skills in reception classes such as phonics. Whenever possible, these should not be for the whole class, as the group is far too big for every child to gain a useful experience from all of the time. For the reception year, some Early Learning Goals and the EYFS Profile scale points relate to children's participation in a variety of group situations in *PSED* and *CLL*, so making observations on their responses, interests and how fully involved they are will be valuable.

Incidental 'catch as you can' observations

These are observations about things which catch your attention that you were not involved in and they often highlight a small, but important step. I usually call these as 'catch-as-you-cans', as this describes exactly how they come about. This is when self-adhesive labels, Post-its or notepads really come into their own – you need to have them with you at all times, at the ready, just in case! 'Catch-as-you-cans' can happen at any time of day – for example, the way one child helped another as they were washing their hands for lunch. Sometimes a child who is shy or new to English who rarely seems to communicate in the setting will be much more communicative when in a small group of peers.

> **Evidence: 4/1**
>
> **Rebecca**, 9 months
>
> Sat in front of the mirror smiling at her image and showing signs of excitement, waving her arms.
>
> **Assessment**: *what does this show about the child's learning and development?*
>
> Excited by and responding to reflection.
>
> **Areas of learning**: *PSED, CLL, KUW*
>
> **Implications for planning**: *what next?*
>
> More play with mirrors of different dimensions and peepbo games.

Evidence: 1/10

George, 2 years 5 months

In home corner, *'I need a baby to feed her! I need a chair for the baby.'* Mixes flour and spoons it onto the plate, adds water. Tells me *'I need more water'* then later *'I need more flour.'*

Assessment: *what does this show about the child's learning and development?*

Confident and able to ask for what he wants, and expresses why in his play – to feed the baby. Explores changes in materials.

Areas of learning: *PSED: DA, SD; CLL: LCT; CD; KUW*

Implications for planning: *what next?*

Continue to organise home corner so children can have real materials to play with (flour/water).

Evidence: 5/4

Elishama, 3 years 2 months

Coming along the corridor after a group time, saw J, smiled at him and held out her hand towards him. They then walked along together.

Assessment: *what does this show about the child's learning and development?*

Elishama has only just started in the nursery, but is already building good relationships with other children through gesture.

Areas of learning: *PSED: DA, SD*

Implications for planning: *what next?*

Continue to support relationship-building between the new children.

Jordan, 4 years 11 months *(J has an Individual Education Plan, supporting the staff to plan for his additional needs in language development)*

Evidence: 9/02

J stood at an empty table with S and pretended to sell ice creams. He had a bottle with a sparkly straw in it, held it out and said *'Ice cream, ice cream'* as his friends walked past.

Assessment: *what does this show about the child's learning and development?*

Jordan is beginning to get more involved with other children in role play: his language is developing in order to help him do so.

Areas of learning: *CLL, CD*

Implications for planning: *what next?*

Ensure adult involvement in role play for Jordan, to assist him to join in (plan this for next week on daily sheet).

Informal conversations and discussions with children

Informal conversations with children anytime and anywhere can provide excellent evidence of learning. This does not mean just conversations with verbal children. A conversation is a two-way communication and can be conducted completely through gesture, expression and eye contact. In making the assessment the following questions might be useful:

Did the child, practitioner or another child initiate the conversation?

How did the child use language: e.g. through gesture, individual words, any new vocabulary, forming sentences?

What type of language was used – e.g. naming objects, giving explanations or descriptions, asking questions?

How did the child express feelings and opinions?

How did the child convey understanding about the subject matter?

Evidence: 8/3

Billy, 4 years 0 months

In role play: *'Do you know what? I'm going to Africa.'* He is holding a map and scans his finger over it: *'I'm gonna go all the way over to Africa. Here –* (points to map) *– it's hot – I got a coat and a hat and a map and there's crocodiles – I'm not brave!'*

Assessment: *what does this show about the child's learning and development?*

Demonstrates good awareness of geographical knowledge – heat, crocodiles, Africa, and able to apply and express this well in play.

Areas of learning: *CLL: LCT*; *KUW, sense of place*

Implications for planning: *what next?*

Continue to build upon Billy's understanding, and use him to help other children in this!

Recordings

Whether using digital, disposable or old-fashioned film cameras, video or audio recording technology, these are excellent ways of recording evidence of learning. They can substitute or complement a written observation, but will need to be dated and sometimes require information about the context. After the event, as part of the assessment, share the recording or photographs with the children and note what they say or feelings they express. These will add to your own reflections.

> *Always ensure you have explicit written permission from parents and children (where possible) for photos and video, specifying how the photos will be used (in records and/or on displays in school or setting). Additional permission will need to be sought should the recording or photo be taken out of the setting (e.g. for training purposes).*

The following example provides a significant learning story about a child persevering in perfecting her own skills.

A Learning Story

Fig. 4.2

Evidence *(first written observation):* 31/3

Elishama, 4 years 7 months

E is hula-hooping with two hoops. *'Look, look! First I learned how to do it with one hoop and now I can do it with two!'*

Practitioner asked her to count as she did it: *'See how many you can count to as you keep the hoop going.'* She counted up to 81!

Assessment: *what does this show about the child's learning and development?*

E has been keen to return to this activity frequently over last couple of weeks. She asks us to make sure we get the hoops out. She is really practising to build up her skills and is able to be very skilful in this. Concentrated, persevering, determined to improve her physical skills.

Areas of learning: *PD; PSED: DA, PSRN*

Implications for planning: *what next?*

Ensure Elishama is able to continue to practise her skills and to teach others (including the adults!) how to do it.

The practitioner's view:

E was really proud of her achievement, which she had learnt at the weekend. She asked for hoops so that she could show her friends. Progressed to using 2 hoops by the end of the first week and encouraged others to learn too.

The child's view

Later, looking at the photos, she said: *'I was doing hula hoops really long . . . and I can do it with loads of hula hoops too.'*

Adult: *'How many?'*

E: *'Three!'*

Adult: *'And how did you learn to do it?'*

E: *'A and my cousin N showed me.'*

Adult: *'So how do you do it?'*

E: *'We have to hold it on and keep it on. If you don't want it to stop you have to bend down . . . I just go round.'*

Observations from parents

Observations from parents at home will help to give a fuller picture of the child. In Chapter 5, George's mother describes how she contributed to George's profile book.

Fig. 4.3

Evidence: 12/3/07 Drew this at home (Figure 4.3)

Benjamin, 4 years 5 months

Drew a train with all his friends on board.

Assessment: *what does this show about the child's learning and development?*

First time he has drawn in such detail – notice sun above and track below.

Areas of learning: *KUW; CD*

Implications for planning: *what next?*

Continue to build his confidence in expressing himself through drawing, painting, etc.

Samples

Samples of evidence include photos of something a child has produced (for example: made a den, a pattern, painting, block building) as well as significant mark-making, drawings, emergent writing, art work, etc. Remember that to make sense and be useful, each sample needs to be analysed. Every child's collection of samples is likely to be different, as the child's achievements are individual.

Fig. 4.4

Evidence: 19/9

Savannah, 4 years 9 months

Three Billy Goats Gruff writing and drawing sample (Figure 4.4)

Assessment: *what does this show about the child's learning and development?*

Using letters and letters shapes she knows to write in *joined up cursive writing!* Good sense of story as able to 'read back' to me. Good attention to detail in her drawing.

Areas of learning: *CLL, CD*

Implications for planning: *what next?*

Continue supporting her on phonic awareness, linking sounds and letters.

Fig. 4.5

Evidence: 13/10 (Figure 4.5)

Bailey, 4 years 10 months

After the maths session where we have been writing numbers, Bailey independently wrote her own. *'Look, number 9 and number 10.'*

Assessment: *what does this show about the child's learning and development?*

Beginning to write number and able to read these back.

Areas of learning: *PSRN*

Implications for planning: *what next?*

Ensure she knows the meaning of the numbers.

Two planned, focused observations

Figures 4.6 and 4.7 are two planned, focused observations where the practitioner stood back to watch for a few minutes – they show how much information can be gathered when observing play in this way.

Fig. 4.6a

Child's name: Thiviya, 4 years 11 months   **Date:** 27/3   **Time:** a.m

Observation context Observer: Angela
T was outside playing with blocks with two other children. This play continued to develop over a significant time during the morning after the observation (see Figure 4.6a). 4-minute observation.
Observation: T lines up the hollow blocks in a straight line. At what seems to be the front end, she puts a small block and then places a plank on top – this produces a slope. She places a second plank across, but under the first plank on top of the original block construction. Tells me (in English) *'It's an aeroplane'* then drapes a piece of light fabric over it. *'That's nice now.'* She sits at the front with three other children behind her. The three of them speak in Tamil together. It's clear from the actions and noises that they are on a journey: *'Weee . . ., Ooohh'*, etc
Assessment: *What did you find out about child's learning with regard to any of the following areas of learning? (What was significant for the child?)*

Personal, Social and Emotional Development (*DA and SD*)

High level of involvement in imaginative play with three others, took lead in (1) building the construction for the play to take place, and (2) co-developing the plot for the play.

Communication, Language and Literacy (*LCT* in 2 languages)

Able to describe in English what the object created was and able to give an evaluative statement (*'That's nice now.'*) In Tamil, was able to continue the play with other Tamil speakers, using her first language.

Problem Solving, Reasoning and Numeracy

Awareness of shape and properties of shape demonstrated through fitting blocks together and balancing the planks.

Knowledge and Understanding of the World

Constructs for a real purpose and effectively: i.e. they could sit on it.
Puts object created to a functional use (to develop imaginative play).

Physical Development

Handles blocks safely and with strength; balances them with precision.

Creative Development

Able to express and develop own fantasy play theme; able to involve others in this by taking leading role. Makes use of materials to develop an imaginative idea: aware of how to create an effective but simple symbolic structure.

Child's comment

See above.

What next?

Staff (particularly bilingual assistant when possible) to get involved in the play, to introduce English vocabulary to the children in this group, in line with their play.

Fig. 4.6b A planned observation

Child's name: George, 2 years 6 months **Tom**, 2 years 9 months **Date:** 18/11   **Time:** a.m

Observation: Observer: Sandy.
As this observation is equally about both children, it has been used for both their records.
George with Tom trying to lift trikes onto climbing frame low platform. I ask why they are doing this.
Tom: *'We need to put our bikes in the shed. They're all broken!'*
George: *'They run out of petrol.'*
They stay on the platform for a while and then try to get the trikes down again. I help. They find chalk and start making marks on the trikes.
G: *'There's the petrol.'*
T: *'Put petrol in my bike.'*
G: *'It's all gone.'*
I join in and with my pen make a squishing sound. They both laugh and G says *'put petrol in my bike!'*
Others join in.
T says *'We're having a picnic'* and they move off around the area and end up moving to sand pit.
Assessment: *What did you find out about child's learning with regard to any of the following areas of learning? (What was significant for the child?)*

Personal, Social and Emotional Development (*DA, SD, ED*)

Both children playing collaboratively together, building on each other's ideas. Happy to engage me in it. Happy for others to join in. Clear feeling of confidence and emotional well-being. T being older appears to take the lead.

Communication, Language and Literacy (Language for communication)

Both children use language to express their ideas and carry the play forward. Equally at ease talking with other children as with adult.

Problem Solving, Reasoning and Numeracy

Knowledge and Understanding of the World

T: aware of concept that, if broken, it needs to go to a special place (the shed).
G: gives reasons for what might be the problem.
T and G know that problem can be solved by filling vehicle with petrol!

Physical Development

Able with support to get the trikes onto the platform.

Creative Development

Both equally contributed to the imaginative play, although T took the lead initially and again later in going for a picnic; G took the lead in suggesting the need for petrol.

Child's comment

Shared through putting example into the profile books, with photos.

What next?

Develop garage mechanic's play with the children, setting up an area, with reception desk, clipboards. Get the children to help in creating own garage 'building' (e.g. in the den area, planks to act as ramp for trikes being mended).

Fig. 4.7 A planned observation

What next and next steps

Throughout this chapter, every observation has resulted in some implications for planning. The next step is to ensure the points genuinely do feed into the day-to-day planning for learning and development. However, there are more perspectives about children's learning which are also needed – those of parents and the children themselves. The next chapter looks at how to ensure parents and the children are full participants in the process of assessment. Then Chapter 6 considers how *all* of this information feeds directly into planning.

Points for reflection
- Do you use a mix of methods of observing in your setting? Which types of observations do your staff team find most useful?
- What systems are in place to ensure that observations are analysed and used in planning?

Involving parents, involving children 5

Working closely with parents is vital in early childhood services if we are truly to support every child's learning. Partnership with parents is integral to the role of childminders, by the very nature of caring for babies and children from a very small number of individual families. Most schools and early years settings of all types accept the importance of partnerships with parents. In the best provision, the importance of close collaboration between parents and the setting as a whole is thoroughly understood. Involving parents in the assessment and planning processes is a taken-for-granted aspect of practice.

In spite of national policy prioritising this for many years, a survey by Ofsted published in Spring 2007 on the quality of Foundation Stage practice in 144 settings and schools highlighted that in one third *'practitioners did not include children and parents well enough in assessment'* (Ofsted, 2007). The historical tendency for a one-sided relationship with parents – in which they are told about their child's progress but not invited to be involved – appears to continue. This is often the result of practitioners' inexperience and lack of confidence in talking to parents, and sometimes a lack of understanding of the positive impact on children's learning. In addition, parents may see their child very differently from how she/he is perceived within the setting, resulting in scepticism about parents' views amongst some practitioners. But this is precisely the point: to build a full picture, finding out about how the child is at home is invaluable, especially if this is very different.

The REPEY research (Siraj-Blatchford et al, 2002) noted: *'The most effective settings (where outcomes for children were highest) shared child-related information between parents and staff, and parents were often involved in decision-making about the child's learning programme.'* However, the Ofsted survey five years later showed that *'parents were rarely treated as true partners, but where this did happen there was a discernable impact on achievement'.*

Off to a good start

Involving parents in the assessment process needs to begin *before* the child starts in the setting – through, for example, a home visit and visits for child and parents to the setting. These events are invaluable in helping staff to get to know the children. Every setting is different, so when and how to talk to parents needs to suit circumstances.

> **Luna Elis**, who is two, does not yet go to a nursery setting but does attend parent and toddler stay-and-play sessions. She is being brought up bilingually with two home languages, and English is a third language she hears around her.
>
> Her parents feel that there is significant information they will want to share before their daughter begins, especially about her communication and language development. They will want to discuss the fact that she is shy at first with adults she does not know. They would want to talk about her interests: music, dancing, painting, joining in with the cooking, setting the table meticulously, and dressing herself independently. They need to know that the setting will be prepared to share information with them regularly. *'We would want to know how she is developing relationships with the other children and the adults, what activities she is engaging in and how she manages the routines, whether she is happy and at ease and how she is communicating with others.'* And they will want to be included and involved in every way they can.

The settling-in period for every child must be carefully managed and supportive to both child and parents. Gathering information is key, ensuring that planning is appropriate to really welcome new children and to meet their needs and interests. The Birth to Three Coordinator at Fortune Park Children's Centre told me: *'The home visit is the first step to building the relationship with parents and the child, and this is most important. Not only can we support the child if we work together, but this time helps families to understand our ethos.'* At times of transition from one setting to another, a discussion between parent and practitioners is necessary, even if the child is moving group or class within the same setting. Many settings have a settling-in review for every child, completed by parents and key worker, soon after the child starts.

There are several sources of useful questions to ask parents about their child, and many local authorities and national early years' organisations have devised their own, but Figure 5.1 shows one I developed with a group of practitioners.

Child's Name:

Date of Birth:

Date of Entry: **Age at Entry:**

Languages spoken at home:

For children up to three and beyond, as necessary: information about care routines, feeding, toileting, comforting procedures and aids, particular likes and dislikes.

Names of family members and other significant people close to child:

Any previous experience of being cared for outside the home or by carers other than parents/principal carers:

Does your child have any particular play interests at the moment, or particular toys he/she likes to play with?

What other sort of things does your child show interest in or talk about?

Is your child used to being with/playing with other children and does he/she enjoy this?

How does he/she respond to situations and people who are new to him/her?

Do you think your child's communication and language development is proceeding well?

Does your child enjoy books and listening to stories? Does he/she have any favourite rhymes, stories, DVDs or CDs?

Does your child enjoy and get involved in imaginative-type play and role play, or activities such as building or constructing, matching and counting?

If you have a garden, or when you go to the park, what does your child like to do?

Do you feel his/her physical development is what you would expect for his/her age?

What do you expect he/she will like about the setting or school?

Does your child have any particular fears or worries or dislikes we should know about?

Is there any more information you would like to know about the setting and what your child will be doing here?

Do you have any concerns or worries about your child's development?

Is there any other information you would like us to know in order to help your child settle and be happy?

Fig. 5. 1

Parents Voice

ኩባታብሁ. ንሁዛቋብሁ. ተትሁ፡ ኦቹዝ፡ ፆዝጊ፡ ያፎካሃዝ፡ ውዐፆ
ቀጣጭሁዝ፡ ቆጦጭ ፡ ሁኅፄ፡ ፁታዝ፡ ዐ)ሀሁባ፡ ዝሁ፡ ሁጣሁ፡ ፖሀፖ
ዐ)ፄዝባ፡ ሁታጊዐጭታ፡ ሁታ፡ ዐ)ሁጭ፡ ቋዐግዐዝ፡ ዐ)ሁሁባ፡ ዐታጣ፡ ዐ)ጣጣብ
ታጣ፡ ጥታፆዐታ፡ ጣዐዝዑሁ፡ ሁ) ሁሁታ ዐ)ፆዐ ሁዝ ሁሁታ፡ ዐ)ታጣ፡ ጭፖዝ
ጭብሁ፡ ሁዝሁ፡ ዐዑሁሁ፡ ፆ-ዝታ - ዐ)ፆዐ፡ ታዝፄ፡ ዐ)ሁሁባ፡ ዝሁ፡ ዐዝጭ
ዐዐ፡ ዐዑሁሁ፡ ጭ፡ ዐ)ዐጣዐታብሁ፡ ታሜ፡ ፄፄብ፡ ዐዐዐዑ ፁ፡ ፄታ፡ ፆ ያፎካ
ፅታሁዐባ፡ ታዝታ ፡ ፆዐኄታ፡ ጭብሁ፡ ሁጌፆፖዐ፡ ፁዝባዐሁ፡ ሁዐዐ
ሁሁ፡ ጭ፡ ዐ)ዐጣዐታብሁ፡ ሁዐፆ፡ ዐ)ሁዐ)ሁባ፡ ጭብሁ፡ ታዐፆዐታ፡ ሁዐዑሁሁ
ታ፡ ፆዐኄታ ፡ ሁሁዝታ፡ ዝሁዝፄ፡ ዐ)ታፄብሁ።።

    Samuel when he wack up in the morning
he bersh his tethe he eat his berakfast
he wach Tomas fim and balamory film. he
like raiding his baik he is going the sheool
when he came back the shcool he had the
lanch after ~~the~~ that ~~he~~ ~~step~~ he drink keis
milk after that he slip one/two hours.
when he waek up and he eat his
yogurt or friut he wach a T.U and
he play with his book pooh and tomas. olso
He play with his brather mo̶ses
He gone out in the park he plays with
her firond danial when he came bake
home ~~ae~~ he eat a diner he slipe
This is samual life.

Harris, a three year old, was observed by his nursery staff to have a passion for dinosaurs. His mother also noted this before he started at the nursery. The nursery built on the child's interests, as can be seen in this sequence:

Parent conference comments:

27/1/02 *'Harris likes to play with dinosaurs, dragons, swords and animals. He loves looking at information books and having bedtime stories read to him . . .'*

Observations in nursery (a year later):

7/1/03 Harris is sitting under the climbing A-frame outside. He and all the other children are dressed in thick coats and hats. Harris and another child have taken two small chairs under the A-frame. Harris is now retelling his favourite dinosaur story to another child and discussing the characters in the book. Harris often chooses books to look at and retell. His interest in dinosaurs is never far away.

Building strong reciprocal relationships

The Ofsted survey (2007) noted that it was increasingly common for parents to be involved in the child's 'entry profile', but far less frequent for them to be involved beyond this. A truly reciprocal relationship with parents goes far beyond the settling-in or transition period.

At Fortune Park, strong collaborative relationships with parents are woven throughout the work of the Centre to support the children's all-round development. The profile book is the child's record, openly accessible at all times to parent and child. The Parents' Voice is the front page of the profile book. Some may be written by parents in the mother tongue, others may be scribed for parents but most write them themselves (Figure 5.2).

Parents are encouraged to take their child's profile book home regularly and to contribute to it and, as George's mother Jaqui explains, it is the most important element of the record-keeping process for the parents at the Centre:

'George's profile book is my window to see what he does when he is at nursery. . . . The profile book shows George at his most natural and means that I don't get to miss his progression or special things that he has said or done while he is there. We put photos in his profile book of what he was doing at home, such as making cakes or going out to the park and

the very first time he rode his two-wheeler bike. This gave the nursery an opportunity to follow up what he was doing at home, and what his key worker put in it gave us the opportunity to follow up what he did at nursery.'

Parents are also involved in the day-to-day planning process through the regular reviews of the child's development and progress. At each review they are asked to add their own views and comments.

Parents' role in the Early Years Foundation Stage Profile

At the end of the Reception year, the EYFS Profile is the statutory assessment for every child. The guidance for the Early Years Foundation Stage Profile (EYFSP) states that:

❛ *Practitioners should involve parents from the time when the children arrive in the setting . . . working with them to gain a shared picture of their children.* ❜

Both parents and the children themselves are expected to have a voice in the assessment process.

The EYFSP is the *only* national compulsory summative assessment system with a formal expectation that information from parents and the children's own views have been included. One way to begin to involve parents in this process would be to use the questions in Figure 5.1 when children transfer into the reception year.

Involving the children

One of my principles in Chapter 3 states: *Children must be involved in their own assessment and their voices heard, regardless of age or ability.* There is now much innovative practice involving even the very youngest children in their own self-assessment in Britain, and some are highlighted in this book. But it is by no means universal practice yet.

Why do we need to involve the children?

There are very good reasons for involving children in the assessment process: some are about the positive effect it has on children's learning, development and self-understanding, and others are about respect, value, rights and justice.

First, we know how our own learning is enhanced by being able to critically reflect and express an opinion on how we did, what went well and what could have been better. It is the same for young children. This is why open, accessible records are so important from the start, giving the children the opportunity to reflect back and develop their self-reflection skills. It builds self-esteem as well as deepening understanding.

In Reggio Emilia, pedagogistas document the process of learning as it happens, scribing for the children, taking photographs and video, recording the discussions and the learning. *'It makes visible . . . the nature of the learning process and strategies used by each child . . . It enables reading, revisiting and assessment in time and in space . . .'* (Rinaldi, 2005). Many settings in Britain have adapted these processes to their own context, using them for planning and assessment.

Second, involving children is a rights issue. The UN Convention on the Rights of the Child (UNCRC), which Britain signed in 1991, establishes in law the rights of children. Article 12 addresses children's rights to express an opinion and to have that opinion taken into account, in any matter or procedure affecting the child. Article 13 follows this with the right to seek, receive and share information. Recently, training and support on how to consult and involve even very young children has had a significant influence in many settings (for example, using the Coram Family *Listening to Young Children* materials, 2003). The knowledge that involving children in self-assessment enhances their learning, and the moral imperative in terms of their rights, should be more than enough to convince us that we *must* involve them. As Lancaster (2003) says: *'Babies voices are there for us to hear from birth.'*

From listening to involving

The first step in involving children in assessment is for practitioners to *listen*. When observation practice is well established, as outlined in Chapter 4, then practitioners will be automatically listening to the children. *Listening* in this sense means tuning into all the many ways the children and babies communicate: '. . . *listening not just with our ears but with all our senses . . . to the hundreds, thousands of languages we use to expresses ourselves and communicate . . .'* (Rinaldi, 2005).

The Coram Family *Listening to Young Children* materials, mentioned above, were developed to support consultation with young children, building on a research project on listening to children's perspectives (Clark and Moss, 2001). The research showed that, as well as talking with children in their preferred medium – such as home language, signing or picture exchange for example – a range of techniques may be needed, fitting the pieces together like a mosaic: for example, observing the child's preferences, sharing their profiles or portfolios, looking at photographs and, even with two year olds, giving them child-friendly digital cameras to take photos of things which are significant to them.

As we listen, we need to ensure we *hear*. This means taking note, ensuring the child knows she/he has been heard. It means responding and, potentially, to take action as a result. *Really* listening, as Lancaster's work on listening to young children shows, helps us to question our assumptions and raises our expectations of their capabilities (Lancaster, 2006). Involving children in the assessment process both supports our listening and gives them a voice. The best approach is to make child-friendly, individual portfolios, sharing and frequently discussing them with the children.

Involving the very youngest

Maxilla Nursery Centre, providing integrated care and learning for children from birth to three in London, now closed, began this practice in 1990. Observations of children's development, along with photographs of children involved in learning experiences and, where applicable, their mark-making, were stored in openly accessible folders. Each page was kept in a plastic file pocket, to ensure children's accessibility without damage to the content. The visual elements of the profile made this immediately accessible, even to the babies as young as 6 months. They were frequently shared by staff with parents and children, and were always available and accessible.

In Fortune Park, the profile book described earlier is the route to involving all the children in the assessment process. *'The nature of the profile book invites interaction and participation. They demand to be looked at and shared'* (Driscoll and Rudge, 2005). Sandy, the Birth to Three Coordinator, told me: *'The profile book is a part of the child's day. We put the photos and pictures in with the child. It is built into what goes on daily. It starts at the home visit by taking photographs, and by the time the child starts, the profile book is already prepared.'*

As well as beginning the reflective learning process, this eases the separation process for the child, linking the child's experiences of home and nursery life.

Fig. 5.3 *Samual and his mother are looking at the profile book together*

The staff have noted how the children use the books differently at different ages: *'For the younger children, the profile books are more intrinsically linked to their emotional being.'* Some younger children will carry them around with them: an emotional link to family or significant events which are recorded in the books. For the older children, the profile books *'become representations of their thinking . . . the older child's thought processes become more explicit as the child develops the ability to express his ideas and reflections on learning'* (Driscoll and Rudge, 2005).

Involving the three, four and five year olds

Children need to be *involved* at every stage in their own assessment. These are some useful strategies:

■   Tell them what you are writing.
■   Show them their record and where to find it.
■   Talk to them about any samples or observations you want to add (giving them a photocopy if they also want to take it home).
■   Ensure they can choose their own things to add to the record.
■   Even if the child doesn't respond the first few times you talk to them about their achievements, don't be put off. Continue.
■   Ask open-ended and inviting questions which will require more than one-word responses or yes/no answers, but don't force the child to respond.

In the Foundation Stage Unit in the primary school, the children's folders are accessible to them and their parents, stored in the classroom area on shelves. Through the termly review process, each child has a time one-to-one with her/his key worker to discuss the folder and the achievements documented within. Children talk about what they could do before and what they can do now. They are then encouraged to choose a friend to look through it with too.

This aspect of the timetabled activities is of great significance to the learning of all the children. The following example shows the kinds of conversations and reflection on learning that can take place with older children.

Aisha is five and in the first few weeks of her first term in Reception. After she had looked through her folder with her teacher, she went and found two friends to look at it with her. They showed a high level of interest and engagement. Things of personal significance were keenly shared: *'That's me cuddling my brother!'* The following transcript of part of the conversation between two of the children, both five, shows how such an approach can enhance learning.

Aisha: *'Do you know what this is, Anthony? I did this when Miss Francis* (her teacher) *came to visit me in the nursery.'*

She turns the page, pointing to a card where she has written her name: *'That's my name.'*

Anthony: *'I begin within an A. . . .'*

Aisha: *'A . . . Anthony.'*

Anthony: *'A . . . two As!'*

Aisha: *'Yes, A and a. My name begins with an A.'*

Anthony: *'A and another a? And a 5 – that isn't a letter!'*

Aisha: *'No, that's Emily's phone number!'* Role play in this reception class in all its various guises always made good use of telephones and recording numbers along with telephone messages.

The conversation continued involving all three of the children with cries of *'let me see it . . . let me see all of it!'* and a variety of queries and questions.

Interviewing children about their learning

A more deliberate, planned conversation, such as that described above, is useful in helping older EYFS children to reflect back on their development. It is an expectation for practitioners to record a conversation with the child in the EYFS Profile, but many settings do this more frequently. It can be carried out in a variety of ways suited to the age and verbal development of the child.

With younger children who are not yet verbally competent, or children with additional needs such as language delay and children in the early stages of learning English as an additional language, other ways of gathering their views will be needed, such as those described by Clark and Moss (see page 74). At first, and especially with younger children, the conversation is likely to be about things that are immediate – for example, something they see around them or have just been involved in. Even so, they may reveal what is important to them, at that moment in time, and often this reflects something of a deeper importance in their development. Once children become familiar with this practice and have a better understanding of the vocabulary in the questions, they become more able to reflect on their own learning.

How to do it

In the book *Listening to Four Year Olds*, Jacqui Cousins (1999) interviewed and listened in other less formal ways to more than one hundred four-year-olds. One of her interview techniques involved using a tape recorder in a pretend studio which children had an opportunity to play with, interviewing each other before she began. For many children, particularly for most children towards the end of their time in Reception, an interview can be a special opportunity to sit down with one child and offer her/him your full attention. Often the best strategy is just being willing to listen and to take seriously what they say, by writing it down or recording it. It *does* need to be planned as a part of the planned teaching, or it is likely to be forgotten or pushed out by other demands. It is best to talk to them individually or in a pair, or three at the most. Asking children about themselves in a group may result in the children giving answers similar to each other.

Asking the questions

The following should elicit the kinds of reflective answers you are seeking:

What do you like doing best at home/setting/school?

What do you think you can do now that you couldn't do before/when you were younger?

What do you think you learn (or learn about) at nursery/school?

What do you learn (or learn about) at home?

What do you think you are really good at doing?

What do you find hard to do or don't like to do?

Have you any favourite toys/books/games/DVDs/songs, etc?

Careful framing of the questions will be required, but the important thing is to *try* asking the questions – if there is no response, try changing how you ask the question. Gura and Hall (2000) point out that questions need to be kept to a minimum and, when questions are asked, '. . . *time should be allowed for children to think about how they will answer.*'

In one nursery school, the teacher asked a series of questions, including the question *'What do you learn at nursery?'* She discovered that, of the children she interviewed, not many understood the key word *learn* (Hutchin, 2003). Gura and Hall (2000) make the point that we do not use words such as *learn* and *teach* enough with children in nursery (although I suspect the words are more common in Reception): *'If children's awareness of their own thinking is to develop, they need to hear adults using words like "think", "wonder", "learn", "teach", "imagine" . . . as they play and work with children.'*

In a nursery class, using the child conferencing process, the teacher interviewed **Lily**, aged 4½ years. This is an extract from the interview.

Teacher: *'What do you like best about our nursery?'*

Lily: *'When everybody gives me stories. I like playing with my friends* (names them). *We play babies and we have to catch Conor but we can't because he keeps running away!'*

Teacher: *'What do you think you are learning when you come to nursery?'*

Lily: *'Counting. I have already learnt sharing. I learn my name.'*

Teacher: *'What do you think you are really good at?'*

Lily: *'I am good at painting, I'm good at cutting.'*

Teacher: *'What do you find hard at school?'*

Lily: *'Sometimes it's hard to write my name. I just like playing with everything. You know, at home it's boring and I like coming to school.'*

It is quite clear from this that useful information about the child's learning can be gathered. Building a picture of her own view of her learning helps show what she needs help with and what she feels confident about.

Having open accessible records and creating time to share them with the children, as described in this chapter, together with an ethos and culture of really listening, will help to ensure children are able to fully participate in self-assessment.

Points for reflection
- What do you find works best in your setting for truly involving parents in your assessment processes?
- How do you involve *all* the children in their own self-assessment?

Linking assessment to planning: supporting every child

6

The systematic link between observation, assessment and planning is the key to ensuring every child's learning and development is supported. In Chapter 3, Figure 3.1 (page 33) is used to show how assessment and planning should be linked, and a set of principles designed to underpin the process are discussed. In this chapter, more detail is given on precisely how to link the processes of observing to assessing to planning, thereby ensuring that short-term and medium-term plans are really appropriate to what the children 'at this place in this time' need, to help them develop and progress.

In Chapter 4, the practical procedures of observation and assessment were outlined, and every example included implications for planning. Chapter 5 considered how to involve parents and the children, whatever their ages, in the process. Wherever the child is and whatever the age, the planning sheet may differ, but the process must ensure that the information gained from the analysis of the observations, samples, recordings, information from parents and the child's view do actually feed into planning. Planning may be written in advance, but it *must* be flexible to truly support learning. This cannot be left to chance – a clearly defined system is needed to make this work. As one practitioner said: *'If you don't observe, how can you plan?'*

Linking assessment to planning: day-to-day planning

The purpose of short-term planning is to ensure every child gets the best from their experiences. It must be flexible, based on your detailed knowledge of each child – much of which will be noted in the child's record. Daily evaluation, in one form or another, plays a significant part in ensuring what is provided is responsive to the children. Although there may be a weekly planning sheet, the content will be modified as things develop, through a daily appraisal process, evaluating *briefly* what took place during the day.

Assuming a process as outlined in Chapter 4 is used, it needs to include:

■ Planning points from some of the observations made during the day;

■ Assessing which learning experiences seemed to hold the children's attention most and extended their learning, and which did not go so well;

■ Whether the learning intentions for any specific adult-led activities were met, or what happened instead.

After this quick evaluation, the planning for the following day is adjusted. Usually it is the provision, learning environment or type of activity and the practitioner's role within this that will be changed, not the learning intentions, as the purpose of the evaluation is to *tune* what is provided to the children.

For Samual, aged 2 years 8 months (example on page 54), after he had been involved in an adult-led cooking activity for the first time, the staff felt that the appropriate planning for him, to sustain his interest, should be *'Provide tools such as play knives and scissors with other materials such as clay, playdough and more cooking!'* For Jordan, aged 4 years 11 months (example on page 56), after noticing him involved in role play, the point for planning was: *'Ensure adult involvement in role play for Jordan, to assist him to join in'*. For the first child, the planning meant adjustments to the resources; for the second, to the adult deployment. Both are equally important in making a difference to the children's ability to learn and progress.

Making the time to evaluate

Different types of settings and different circumstances mean that the way that the evaluation is done will vary. A childminder on her/his own with a small group of children at home may find the time to reflect and plan *before* the children arrive in the morning. In a playgroup, nursery class or nursery school, the best approach may be for the team to sit down together for ten minutes at the *end* of the day or session. Some find it better to talk as they are tidying up, and for one practitioner to be given the responsibility to enter the changes onto the planning sheet. This is the approach taken in the Foundation Stage Unit described in Chapter 9. As well as the termly reviews described in the case study, the staff hold daily evaluations as they tidy up at the end of the day, to ensure learning from one day is followed up the next day, and the planning is tailored to the children. Sometimes the main points of the discussion are about individual children or an overview of the day, and often both.

In a Children's Centre or day nursery where the staff work shifts, another way has to be found to gather evaluations from those on different shifts. The evaluation at the end of the day needs to include information from all the staff to feed into what the staff on an early shift will set up the following day. Some practitioners do this verbally, but unless the points are recorded in some way – however briefly – they may not be passed on to other team members. Having a moment to jot down a few notes on the planning sheet at the end of each shift, before practitioners leave, often works best. A similar process will be needed in a reception class for any of the classroom assistants finishing before the end of the school day.

Although in a group setting the discussion may often be the most important element and there is no need to write everything down, in the usual busy day much may be forgotten if it is not recorded. Even if a practitioner works alone with a group of children, having a few minutes to plan for the next day, based on what has taken place today, is vital.

Linking assessment to planning: reviewing children's records

The second level of linking assessment to planning is less immediate but equally important. This involves reviewing every child's record regularly, in order to consider what has been collected, address any implications for planning not yet addressed, and note any gaps (for example, in an area or aspect of learning). In this way you can make a more general assessment of the child's progress and development whilst ensuring any planning points are not overlooked.

In the Practice Guidance (3.2), the EYFS recommends the following:

6 *Involve children in planning the week's activities by asking them what they would like to do and adapt your own ideas to incorporate theirs. This enables plans to be developed and delivered in ways that are meaningful and relevant to children.* 9

This may sound daunting, especially with younger children in the age range, but is very worthwhile: when children have access to their own records, as discussed throughout this book, it is an important time for child and adult together, planning next steps. I recommend reviewing the records on a rolling programme, choosing a few children per week, ensuring the necessary information from these is fed into the following week's plans. Every week arrange a time to review a small number of records, chosen from the whole group in rotation. Review the record in the room *with the child*, as described in Chapter 5. It should take 5–10 minutes per child, timetabled into the normal day.

This process has two purposes. First, it gives you the *time to review* the record and summarise what you know about the child, and to identify any gaps in the record for any areas of learning. Second, it *involves the child*, giving the child time to reflect on his or her own development and learning, celebrating achievements and deciding what next. This is such an important time for the child. In some of the settings in the case studies, the children's involvement in the review process has countless benefits. I recommend that whatever the setting, as a minimum, every child's record should be reviewed in this way once per term. As one teacher, Angela, said: *'It's a good opportunity to have some one-to-one time with the children. You find you get most language from them at this time and there just aren't enough opportunities for that.'*

From reviewing to planning

Using a format such as the one below can be helpful in summarising priorities for learning and how these are to be planned.

Child's name: Date:
What next? *(learning priorities)* * * *
Planning: *play opportunities, learning experiences and strategies for staff*

What you are planning is a learning opportunity you will be *offering* to the child. It is not a matter of compelling the child or assuming that, because the child did take up what was planned, he or she has necessarily made a leap in development as a result. Some settings, especially in schools, prefer to review all the children in the same week. However, reviewing a small number of records each week makes the link to planning more immediate and manageable. Here is a description of the process used with the 'birth to threes' children at Fortune Park:

From reviewing to planning

'The reviews of children's interests, development and progress from our observations and parents' views which we discuss at our co-key worker meetings feed directly into the planning for the following week and subsequent weeks. But we also plan for all of the children, as there will only be some children's records reviews – usually a review for each child would take place perhaps once every three months.

'In order to make sure we plan for every child, we have a very simple format, where we summarise in a few words something about each child in our key groups – their interests, needs and schemas we have observed during the week. Next to it is the 'adult's role' – what we will do to ensure we plan for that child. Every key worker writes one of these *before* the planning meeting, and then what we are actually going to plan to do is discussed at the meeting.

'Our planning isn't about the activities – making dough, or playing with water – because these things go on all the time: it is about how we are going to offer it and anything additional we will offer too.'

Setting learning priorities or targets for older children

Increasingly in schools, it is likely that teachers are setting learning priorities for their children. This is an aid to planning, part of the assessment for learning process, ensuring the children know what the 'target' learning is for them, but it also helps to track progress. These learning priorities need to be individual, geared to the child's specific needs. They must be achievable and relevant to the child's interests and learning styles, which may mean helping to extend these in new directions.

Birth to threes: Interests/needs/schemas for weekly planning

Name of staff member: Kate   **Date:**

Name of child: Charlotte	Adult's role	Name of child: Daniel	Adult's role
C is now beginning to build friendships with other children – showing particular interest in Florence who is the same age. Keen on riding bikes and playing hide and seek and chasing game. Loves painting, beginning to get involved in role play.	Support her in group activities such as role play, to encourage relationships, dancing, music Take photos of other children for her Profile Book.	D very interested in looking at books, by himself as well as with adults. Loves being involved in music sessions – especially the piano. Recently lots of interest in mark-making on the whiteboard and outside. Very proud of using the toilet by himself. Beginning to join in role play with others	Remind D to use the toilet regularly every half hour or so. Support him in role play. Ensure more music sessions and more time on the piano, help him to listen to the different sounds he can make.

Name of child: Joe	Adult's role	Name of child:	Adult's role
Very sociable – loves company of other children. Now he has become mobile he is becoming very independent and will move away from adult to explore. He is able to use some Makaton signs for animals.	As his key person I need to know the Makaton signs he knows, so I can introduce others! Talk to his mum about this. Introduce some sit-on wheel toys outside for him.		

Fig. 6.1 Part of a weekly planning sheet

In *Observing and Assessing for the Foundation Stage Profile* (Hutchin, 2003) an example from a nursery school is given with one child's 'targets', showing how these are followed up through the school's review processes. In this school the key workers wrote reviews on children's progress in every area of learning twice per year. This is done on a rolling programme. Figure 6.2 shows some of the targets from the reviews for the child, as well as what the nursery will do to support him.

Date	Targets
November (two months after starting at nursery)	• To part happily from Mum and Dad • For nursery to provide opportunities for him to develop English and support his home language (through Arabic tapes and alphabet) • To identify and name colours and shapes in English • To access all areas of the curriculum
March	• Share core story books at nursery in English and borrow books from school library. Mum to continue using Arabic for speaking and writing at home • Count in sequence to 10+ • Extend his use of computer: e.g. using keyboard
November	• Retell familiar stories using remembered words and phrases; make connections between spoken word and print • Write most letters in his name • Count with 1:1 correspondence to 10
March	• Continue to retell stories with books/props and acting them out, building on existing repertoire • Help him to develop awareness of rhyming words and linking sounds and letters, both when he writes and when we scribe for him, building on his enthusiasm for writing • Encourage Arabic writing and use of Arabic in the nursery

Fig. 6.2

In another school, in the reception class, Dilwen, the teacher, reviewed her children's records once every half-term. In this school there was always a literacy and mathematical target, and the third target was usually chosen in discussion with the child. Children, especially in Reception, can be very good at devising their own meaningful targets, once they are given the opportunity to be regularly involved in a self-assessment process. One example quoted showed Anna choosing her own targets: in one term it was *'to climb a rope'* and a few months later *'to make a cake all by myself'*. The teacher added the literacy and mathematical targets in the presence of the child: in one term, for example: *'To write a sentence and use a full stop'* and in the next term: *'To add on numbers 0–9 mentally or using fingers'*. The targets or learning priorities then inform not just the next week's planning: some will steer the medium-term plan for weeks to come, especially those which are shared by a number of children.

Linking assessment to planning: medium-term planning

The final link between assessment and planning described here is *medium-term* planning. This may not be appropriate everywhere, or necessarily used – it is more usual in a school setting. The medium-term planning provides the link between the long-term broad curriculum entitlement to the specific group of children for whom it is meant, turning the entitlement into practical possibilities tailored to the children, as a result of the reviews of the records. Sometimes it may be for a half-term, a month, or even shorter. It means building on children's interests and needs, as well as offering other things you want them to experience and find out about. Figure 6.3 illustrates how the medium-term planning needs to be formulated. As with the under-threes setting described above, if not all children's records have been reviewed in the period leading up to the review, more general points will need to be included for them too.

Medium-term planning, for those who use it, then feeds into the weekly overview in the short-term plans, which are adjusted daily as described above, by the evaluations and information from observations.

Summarising development and progress

The daily evaluations and termly or half-termly reviews of each child's record ensure an effective system of assessment *for* learning. The same processes should apply in every type of setting, but they will look different, tailored to the context. This forms the ongoing

The Influences	The Process	What it looks like
• The specific group of children it is designed for: their interests, preferences, capabilities and needs – their possible lines of development	***Creating the medium-term overview*** *Before the planning meeting:*	➢ What you intend the children will be learning and developing ➢ Broad outline only of possible experiences and opportunities
• Evaluation of what has gone on before • The long-term planning framework (based on EYFS Learning and Development sections appropriate to the children's age groups) • For older children, any special events/ seasonal features, etc	Review at least some of the children's records Then hold a planning meeting with all practitioners involved	➢ The possible provocations or interesting ideas to use as starting points, and how practitioners will be involved in supporting play ➢ Resourcing the learning environment inside and outside

Fig. 6.3

record-keeping process. From time to time, *summative* records are also needed. In nursery settings and with childminders this will be at points of transition: when moving to a new setting or school. At the end of the Early Years Foundation Stage this will be the EYFS Profile, used for transition to Year 1. These summative records will be the topic of the Chapter 8, which also looks at tracking progress. The next chapter provides some case studies of how learning is supported in exciting and stimulating ways in a range of settings.

Points for reflection

- How do you ensure that what you have found out about children's learning and development each day feeds into your planning?
- How often do you review each child's record or learning diary? How do you use the review to plan the 'next steps' for each child?

Effective practice in action: some case studies

7

The purpose of this chapter is to share some of the ways that a range of early years settings have developed their practice to support every child's learning through their ongoing assessment and planning processes. These 'case studies' show a breadth of different types of settings, from childminder to schools. There are so many effective systems and processes in early years settings and all will be at least slightly different, even when meeting the same set of principles such as the EYFS principles and those set out in Chapter 3. The case studies here are not a representative sample of practice, but describe individual settings where practitioners have developed their processes for observing, assessing and planning according to their different circumstances and staffing arrangements. What they have in common is a belief in building planning from what children *can* do, and the importance of observing.

The most important criteria for choosing these settings is that they represent reflective practitioners who are open to new ideas and keep their approaches under review, developing them in the light of their evaluations. Some of the settings have been greatly influenced by the pre-schools of Reggio Emilia in Italy and by the New Zealand early years curriculum, *Te Whariki*, described in Chapter 2. Others have been particularly influenced by the *Listening to Young Children* programme (Coram Family, 2003), as a way of making sure children's voices are heard and listened to, and especially that they are involved in their own assessment. As explained in Chapter 5, the UN Convention for the Rights of the child has been particularly influential in this development. Involving parents in the assessment and planning processes has also been particularly important in these settings.

A Sure Start children's centre: birth to three provision

Fig. 7.1

Fortune Park Children's Centre was already a designated Early Excellence Centre when it became a Sure Start Children's Centre in 2006. As well as a range of family support and health services for families with children under five, it provides inclusive education and care for 65 children from birth, for 49 weeks of the year. It is soon to incorporate the reception year from the primary school on the same site. Their successful assessment and record-keeping practice, particularly in ensuring the voice of the child and voice of the parent are heard, has been widely shared since 1999, when it featured in *Right from the Start* (Hutchin, 1999). For the Head and her senior management team, reviewing and reflecting on practice are essential.

As the Birth to Three Coordinator, Sandy, said: *'We have gradually developed our processes over time. The message has been "start with the* child". It really works when you do that. But we do need to keep reviewing what we do – to come together to discuss "Is it working well?" What do we need to change and what do we need to prioritise?'

The Head of Centre, Caron, feels that with a complex staff team, as in a Children's Centre, some aspects of their work are essential to be effective: 'Most important is not deviating from our ethos and vision. What does our ethos look like when we consider children's behaviour? What does our ethos look like for children with special needs? We need to constantly share our strategies to develop consistency across all the teams. It takes time to evolve and time to really understand how best to do what we are trying to achieve.'

Three aspects of the record-keeping process feed into planning: information from parents, observations by staff and the child's view.

Profile books

The *profile book* is the child's personal portfolio which begins at the child's home visit. As Sandy told me: 'The profile books are very individual – no two profile books are alike. They are living working documents and totally the ownership of the child.' They are used throughout the day, stored totally accessibly to even the very youngest at all times, a part of the Centre's enabling environment for all children. This is part of listening to young children from birth onwards: 'Every aspect of a child's life is represented in the profile book. Learning that takes place at home or at nursery is represented, as well as what a child has to say about it' (Driscoll and Rudge, 2005).

The parents' role in them is described in Chapter 5. They contain photographs and samples, such as the child's own mark-making, with information about the context, quotes from the children and the date. 'They bring the observation diaries to life. Sometimes there will be a sequence of photos – these become stories about an event which was particularly important for the child.'

Observation diaries

Each key worker maintains an observation diary for each child in their group, where observations, reviews and summaries are kept. 'The observations are a necessary part of the process – this is what we reflect on as we decide on possible next steps for the children.' Two types of observations are used: the quick notes written as staff work with the children, and the longer narrative observations.

They also make use of video, particularly in their work with parents, providing an opportunity for staff and parents together to reflect on how adults can support children's learning. *'One morning a week, a group of parents are invited in to stay and play with their children and we video this session. The following week the video is played and we discuss it with the parents, looking at what the children and the adults are doing. It has helped everybody to understand more about children's learning and our role in supporting this. These are really powerful sessions.'*

From observing to planning

The cycle of assessment to planning works really well in the Centre, through regularly reviews of children's records and daily evaluations, all of which feed into planning. There are fuller explanations of the process in Chapter 5 and 6.

Long-term benefits to the children

The long-term effect of these profile books on children's lives was very much in evidence when the Centre held a celebration event for its 10th anniversary. Children and families who had been at the Centre over the years were invited to come. Many of the parents and children documented how important the Centre has been to their lives, and for the children the profile books were particularly significant. Many of the children had kept these, and some continued to update then – even ten years later.

A childminder

Janet has many years' experience as a childminder, caring for children in her own home. Most of the children begin in her care as small babies. Taking on board the EYFS poses no problem, as her work focuses so clearly on the four key themes: unique child, positive relationships, enabling environment and learning and development. The positive interactions the young children receive through her care provide an enormous support to their development. Relationships with the families of many of the children continue to such an extent that some children stay with her after school or in the school holidays. Much of the time she is with two other childminders in her house, working together with all the children. Her personal philosophy underpins her practice: start with the child and provide responsive care.

Janet finds her work immensely rewarding: *'I love watching the children grow and develop, achieving things they couldn't do yesterday, knowing that you and their parents have been a part of that process. I love talking with them and watching them, the way they explore things and question. The way they see things is so interesting.'*

Recording children's development

Janet feels that the only reason to record anything about the children's development and learning is, first, for the parents and, second, for the children themselves. Her main form of recording is through taking photos – which she does frequently. This provides just the kind of record that parents and the children need.

Janet told me: *'I started taking photographs of the children about 12 years ago, documenting their learning and development from when they started with me until they were about 18 months or so. Then I gave the child and the family an album full of photographs as a gift just about their child. Parents loved it so much they wanted me to continue. The children love them too. The older children who still come often look at the photos and discuss them with me.'*

At the time of my interview with Janet, she did not write observations, but is highly observant. For example, she observes and notes the children's schemas and the need to plan to 'feed' them. The photos she took of George and his fascination with rotation and enclosure are mentioned in Chapter 2.

'It is so different working in your own home from working in a setting. My relationships with the parents and the children are so strong. We talk every day about how their child has been and what we have done. They do not want pieces of paper telling them this – the important thing is that we have built a close and professional relationship. . . . There is nothing more precious than leaving your baby with someone. What parents want is you to talk with them, to tell them about how their child was, not a bit of paper'.

Planning

Janet does not make lengthy formal written plans, but she does plan. What she provides for the children is entirely based around ensuring children are learning in a fun way through high-quality interaction and the provision she makes for their play, inside and outside. Her planning builds on children's particular interests, giving them a wide range of experiences in all areas of learning, but in a really informal way.

Her garden includes a pond in a fenced-off area which she takes the children to visit: *'Next week we are planning to look at bugs – first ladybirds, then bees. This has come completely from the children – it is from their interests, but more because of their uncertainties about insects! They tend to be quite frightened of them when they are in the garden, so it seems a really good time to be looking at them more closely!'*

A children's centre

Tunstall Nursery School is one of the schools featured in *Observing and Assessing for the Foundation Stage Profile*. As always, practice changes and develop over time, but the effective processes for assessment and planning have remained in principle the same. In March 2007 the school was designated a Children's Centre. An important part of its provision is a Family Room where parents/carers with children from birth to rising-4 are able to *'come along, relax and play with their children'*. The principles, practice and expectations of the EYFS are reflected in the planning and organisation of the sessions in the Family Room, just as they are in the nursery school part of the Centre.

Every child throughout the Centre has a 'Special Folder' which documents the significant developments she/he is making at nursery and at home, through photographs, samples, captions and the child's own comments. The folders are kept on low, open shelves, accessible to the children and parents. Each folder has the child's photograph and name on the cover and, as a starting point – linking nursery with home – children are encouraged to bring in a favourite photo or two from home. They also use their local authority's Record of Achievement format, writing observations onto sticky labels and adding them to the children's records under the appropriate areas/strand of learning. Each member of staff is key worker to a group of children, responsible for developing the folders of the children in her/his group.

A visit to Reggio Emilia by the deputy head, Sue, influenced the development of documenting children's learning in the nursery. It has been further influenced by Margaret Carr's (2001) Learning Stories. The Family Room and nursery use digital cameras to complement the observations, documenting significant moments in

Jacob is using large pieces of paper and thick felt pens to make marks and draw. He has made his own representations of fire, smoke and fire engines.

Physical and Creative Development

Fig. 7.2 A learning story: Jacob's drawing

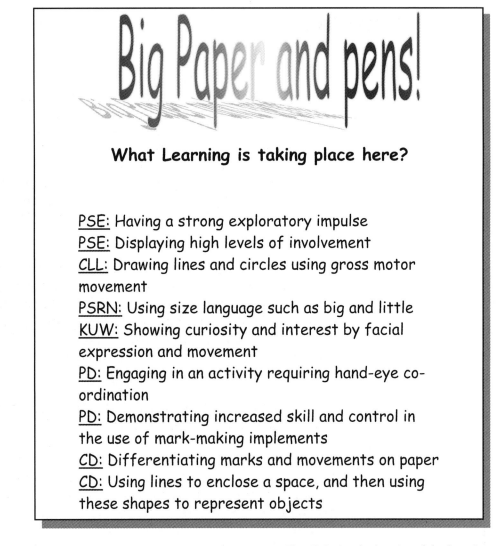

Fig. 7.3 Analysing Jacob's drawing

children's learning as they happen. The stories are written up on the computer with the children from the observational notes taken at the time, alongside the digital photographs. The Head of Centre, Penny, feels strongly that documenting progress in this way is a really meaningful process which can be shared with child and parents and other visitors to the school – much more informative than tick sheets or checklists.

A day nursery

Nutfield is a private day nursery, on the ground floor of a private house, which takes children as babies until they go to school. The nursery can have up to 40 children at any one time, but as many of the children are part time, there are 100 children on roll altogether. There is a large, well-established garden and dedicated play areas outside for different age groups. Outdoor play is an important part of every child's day. The ethos is one of positive relationships and an emphasis on learning through play, supported by caring staff. As Emma, the manager, said: *'A priority when it comes to planning is building on children's interests. We are interested in what interests the children.'*

The key workers keep individual development folders for each child – beautifully presented records which contain the ongoing notes that staff make on the children, along with photographs of the child in action. There is an emphasis on building good-quality records on all aspects of development and learning for every child. Most of the observations in the nursery are incidental 'catch-as-you-can' observations written on Post-it notes.

In the 18 months–3 years group, the room leader, Emily, has developed a good system for linking what the staff have observed to the planning. By displaying the Post-it note observations on the wall under the aspects – such as A Skilful Communicator or Competent Learner – of *Birth to Three Matters*, they can see at a glance the observed developments of the children and any gaps. The link to what needs to be planned is clearly visible. On the planning sheet, under the particular planned objectives, children's initials are added, so staff can see the possible next steps for the children. Planning may include planning to observe – a note to remind staff to observe a particular aspect of development for a child.

Ally, the provider, sees the EYFS as a golden opportunity to review the successes of the nursery and areas for development, and the staff I spoke to agree. As Emily said: *'It is a positive change for us, much easier than having two different documents.'* For the three to fives, the link between the observations and planning is an area that Ally and the staff are aware needs some further thought and development. The introduction of the EYFS will help them with this.

A really successful recent development has been getting parents more involved. As a day nursery for working parents, open twelve hours a day, it has been hard to get parents deeply involved. But as Ally told me: *'We have started planning around "key dates" such as events, festivals and celebrations in a much more obvious way, asking parents to get involved in helping us with resources. We usually link a roleplay scenario into it as well as a range of activities such as cooking. We then take lots of photographs of the events to share with parents. Parents are much more involved now. We also have an open afternoon on the last day of every month when parents can come and join us for the afternoon. We share the records with them then too.'*

An infant school nursery class

St Saviour's Infant School takes children from 3 years up to the age of 7. The nursery class practice is at the forefront of finding ways to document the children's learning, using new technologies to capture it, share it with the children and parents and, together, reflect on it. The teacher and staff team's approach to documentation have been strongly influenced by the class's involvement in a local authority-supported Creativity project entitled '5×5×5 = creativity'. (Bath Spa University, 2002 ongoing.)

There are several aspects to ensuring learning is visible here. Every child in the Foundation Stage has a *learning diary*. This is a portfolio where photographs, observations of various kinds and samples of the children's creative work are kept accessible to parents and children. Recently the nursery team has developed a digital portfolio where the children have their own personal folder on the computer – with their photo as their personal icon. These folders can be accessed by the children during the session, and the images and clips within them are frequently explored by the whole nursery together, both children and adults.

The teacher, Ed, said: *'The digital portfolio has created a reflective record for every child using PowerPoint. It includes video clips and documentation of significant moments that have been jointly recorded by practitioners and the child, thus making it more interactive than the paper version of the learning diary.'*

Every week there is a 'weekly review', an interactive group session with the children and teacher, using a large computer screen to show significant moments and events which have been recorded during the week on video or digital camera. The teacher and children discuss and annotate them together. This presents a wonderful opportunity for children to reflect on themselves and their learning. Ed told me: *'It builds a group culture, where the children are so much more aware of each other and begin to use each other as experts.'* This is democratic education in action, empowering and motivating to the children.

There are also plenty of opportunities on an individual level to discuss and review significant learning events as they happen. *'We use a stylus and tablet to write the children's comments and our own directly onto the PowerPoint slides of photographs – often of significant things which have happened during the week or other provocations to get a discussion going. This is very immediate, shared with the children using a projector. Parents can also watch these group sessions as a 'live' transmission of this session on the screen facing out through the window in the nursery garden. They too are watching the annotation process as it happens – words and drawings appear on the photos, representing the children's ideas.'*

Figure 7.4 shows the outcome of one such discussion on a photograph taken a few months earlier, showing a very dark storm cloud looming over the sunny but wintry outdoor garden at the nursery – a good stimulus for a discussion.

The aim of these interactive sessions is to develop children's thinking skills, as well as documenting learning. Children see their thoughts written down as they happen, greatly increasing their awareness about literacy (that writing is talk written down) but also enabling them to reflect on their thoughts when it is read back to them.

Not all of the documentation is state-of-the-art technology in this form. There are other tools such as large cardboard sheets where photos are stuck and annotation is written up immediately – part of the daily reflection which can be shared there and then without the technology.

Child-initiated learning is now well established throughout school as a key way to develop children's creativity and thinking skills. Each year group has a time when children are given opportunities to pursue their own research, explorations and investigations within the classroom environment. The nursery was recently involved in a National Strategies Foundation Stage project on documenting young children's learning (DfES Standards website 2007), and the whole school is involved with several projects developing children's thinking skills.

Fig. 7.4 As the children look at and discuss the photo projected on the wall from the computer, their teacher writes up their comments using a tablet and stylus

A primary school foundation stage unit

Bond Primary School in the outer London suburbs has a profile common to schools in many areas of London. In the nursery and reception classes, 70 per cent of the children have English as an Additional Language, and at the time of my visit ten children in the group of 90-plus were on the Action Plus stage of the SEN Code of Practice.

Lisa, the Foundation Stage Coordinator, and the team provided many examples of observations and a case study for *Observing and Assessing for the Foundation Stage Profile*, in 2003. Recently the nursery and reception classes have combined into a Foundation Stage Unit. Within the rich learning environment in the open-plan classroom and outdoor areas, the organisation of staff enables some staff to act as facilitators to children's self-initiated learning (called 'interactors') whilst others are involved in focused activities with small groups of children, inside and outside. The overall impression is of busy, involved children independently working and playing, with or without staff, in small groups or alone.

The observation, assessment and planning processes

All staff in the team observe the children and most of the observations are quick 'catch-as-you-can' notes, written down on self-adhesive 'stickers'. Other evidence is collected through photographs and samples such as children's drawing and writing. Each child has their own portfolio for samples and photographs in a ring-bound folder – the children's 'special work folders'.

The teachers and nursery nurses take responsibility for the record-keeping for a group of children. In addition to the folders, an observation diary is compiled for each child, consisting of the observations collected over time filed under areas of learning. There is also a system for tracking progress in learning and development, using a learning map consisting mainly of the Stepping Stones and Early Learning Goals. Only a few minimal changes have been necessary to update this to the Development Matters statements from the EYFS.

Involving parents and the children in the assessment processes is an important feature of the unit. They all have access to the special folders, which are stored in an area of the room. Parents know that they can ask to see their child's observation diary at any time.

There is a well organised system for reviewing children's record. A time is set aside for the staff member responsible for a group to look through, review and discuss the record with each child individually in her group, in rotation, at least once per term. This gives each child a significant opportunity for a *personal* time with an adult to reflect on his or her own development and achievements. After this, the adult suggests the child finds some friends to share the folder with, thus supporting their developing relationships and respect for each other. A transcript of one such conversation appears in Chapter 5. Children were thrilled to bring their folders to me, as a visitor, to look through with them. The conversations were about what they felt was most significant to them. This was often something quite different from what I, as an outsider, might have perceived as significant to the child's learning, giving a real insight into the child's feelings, thought processes and ways of learning.

Once the review with the child has taken place, parents are invited to a parent review meeting to talk through the child's achievements and discuss future plans. It is a time when the parents look through the folder and the observation diary with their child. Lisa told me:

Fig. 7.5

'The children love sharing their folders with their parents. It often reinforces what has been discussed with the staff member as children are aware of their own strengths and next steps. It also provides a really good opportunity for us to talk to the parents about what we do, such as how we teach reading and writing – and we have examples there in front of us: their child's own work.'

Points for reflection

- Each of the settings described here has taken a slightly different approach to documenting children's learning and development. Does your setting use similar approaches to any of these?

- The settings in this chapter also have different strengths to celebrate and areas for development to work on, in order to ensure every child's learning is fully supported. What are your own strengths and areas for development?

Supporting transitions and tracking progress 8

The EYFS refers to learning as a continuous journey. This 'Learning Journey' '. . . is unique to each child because it is built up from their individual mix of life experiences' (3.2, p. 1 in depth). The most important influences on children's life experiences is what goes on at home, but attendance at a setting will also be influential and experience of this can vary greatly from one child to another.

Rebecca, for example, began part-time in a day nursery a few days a week at the age of six months. Finn began at about the same age with a childminder a few days a month, to fit with his mother's work pattern, and then began to attend a nursery once he was two. George began in the Children's Centre when he was two and stayed until he was nearly five, when he began in Reception. Luna Elis will attend a setting for the first time when she is three years and two months, whereas Nicholas has been at home with his mother until he began in the local school reception class at nearly five.

There are broad patterns of development which most children follow, and Figure 8.1 gives us a wonderful insight into how Savannah (at the age of four) sees this. But *how* and *when* is unique to each child:

> *A child does not suddenly move from one phase to another and they do not progress in all areas at the same time* (EYFS Child Development Overview card).

Tracking progress

Tracking children's progress is important. Chapter 6 outlined some practical ways of linking assessment to planning. The cycle from observing to assessing to planning is vital in ensuring children can progress. Let's look at an example of one child's progress, tracked through the ongoing observations collected over her time in school.

Arane was fluent for a three year old in her first language, Tamil, but new to English when she started in the nursery class in a primary

I am a litte I'am Machbiger I am veree biger
bady ICyt wac savannah and I am go ni to
Dee koose I am litte. BOND
PRIMARY

Fig. 8.1 Savannah growing up

school. Her home experiences, with support from the setting, enabled her to make rapid progress in her communication, language and literacy development. At school, the rich learning environment and bilingual support, as well as focused teaching, has supported Arane's speedy development. Not all children's progress will be the same: the practitioners who work with her are well aware that her development is unique to her.

Evidence: 20/01

Arane, 3 years 4 months

Picked up a book and pointed to the words, tapping her finger on the page as adult said each word of a familiar rhyme, *baa, baa, black sheep*.

Assessment: Realises that it is the *words* which are read (not pictures), and is beginning to make one-to-one correspondence between the rhythm of the words and marks on the page.

Implications for planning: *what next?*

Use large rhymes cards with this group of children at rhyme time. Point to words when reading short texts and rhymes with Arane.

Evidence: 23/05

Arane, 3 years 8 months

Went to the registration board and pointed to her own name, smiling.

Assessment: Can read her name from a list of names (several other names start with 'A' in the class!)

Implications for planning: *what next?*

Check if she can read her name in other contexts too, e.g. on pictures, displays, in notes, roleplay, etc.

Evidence: 5/10

Arane, 4 years I month

Looking at a book with an adult, she points to the letter 'A' at the beginning of a sentence. I say *'A for Arane'* and she smiles.

Assessment: Recognises letter A (first letter of her name) independently. Pleased when her achievement is recognised.

Implications for planning: *what next?*

What other letters does she recognise outside the context of her name?

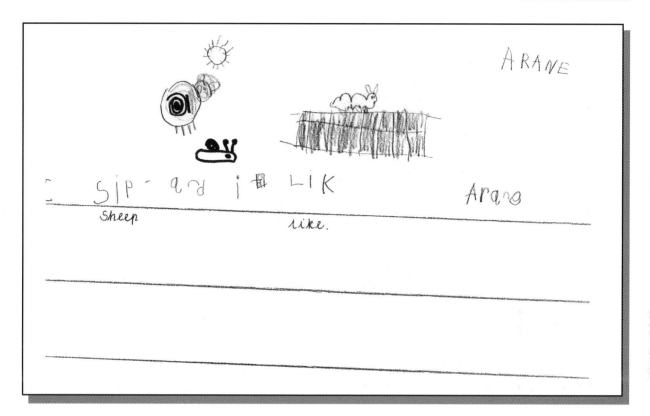

Fig. 8.2

Evidence: 12/6 (see Figure 8.2)

Arane, 4 years 9 months

Independent writing, makes spaces between words, able to write the sounds she can hear in unfamiliar words, and writes '*I*' and '*and*' from memory. Read back her writing to me.

Assessment:

Really gaining in skill and confidence with her writing. It shows how clearly she knows about linking sounds and letters and punctuation.

Implications for planning: *what next?*

Continue to provide a variety of purposes for writing.

Evidence: 13/9 **(see Figure 8.3)**

Arane, 5 years 0 months

Writing about the Three Billy Goats Gruff, Arane independently wrote the sounds she can hear within all the words in her sentence, and puts a full stop at the end. Wrote some familiar words from memory (e.g. *'the'*).

Assessment:

Really gaining in skill and confidence with her writing. It shows her knowledge about linking sounds and letters and punctuation.

Implications for planning: *what next?*

Help her with spacing her words.

Fig. 8.3

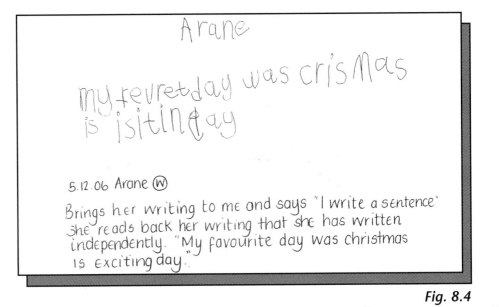

Arane

my fevretday was crismas
is isitineday

5.12.06 Arane Ⓦ

Brings her writing to me and says "I write a sentence"
She reads back her writing that she has written
independently. "My favourite day was christmas
is exciting day."

Fig. 8.4

Evidence: 5/12 (see Figure 8.4)

Arane, 5 years 3 months

Brings her writing to me and says: *'I write a sentence.'* She reads back her writing – this was independent writing. *'My favourite day was Christmas is exciting day.'*

Assessment: Continuing to use her well developed knowledge of phonics in her writing. Confident to share what she has done independently

Implications for planning: *what next?*

Continue to provide lots of purposes and stimuli for independent writing inside and outside.

Evidence: 26.03

Arane, 5 years 6 months

Completely independently wrote out a nursery rhyme for herself, complete with picture.

Assessment: Rhyme was *'Hey diddle diddle'*: she wrote it as: *Heidadidle, Heidadidle,* (she is familiar with the first letters as she knows them from another child's name*), the cat and the veiling'* (here she changed the word *fiddle* to *violin* – so had concept of the instruments and changed the name to what she knew!)

Implications for planning: *what next?*

Offer her and others who would be interested the opportunity to write their own rhyme books to 'publish' in the class.

Smooth transitions

From home to nursery

Positive, supportive relationships will help ensure the children settle well and do not feel bewildered when beginning in a setting. Smooth transitions happen when the uniqueness of every child is taken seriously. Chapter 5 spells out the importance of partnership with parents and how to support the settling-in period for every child. But it is not *just* about being comfortable and at ease.

6 *To foster progress, settings should create an environment that achieves a balance between providing enough of the familiar to reassure, while presenting enough of the new to stimulate and extend.* 9 (EYFS, 3.2)

Continuity in what is planned will help to ensure the children's learning journeys are smooth, without a hiccup in their learning and development.

George started nursery at two years old, in the Children's Centre. His first encounter with his key worker was at the home visit, and by the time he started, his first profile book already contained photographs of him and his family taken during the visit. This helped to ensure a smooth transition from home to nursery. Throughout his time at the Centre, observations were shared with him and his parents through the profile book, to which they also contributed, and the observation diary. Regular reviews ensured that any planning points not picked up through weekly planning, would be followed through. Throughout his record in the 'birth to threes', his interests in cartoon films continued to be important and used by the staff as a vehicle to supporting his learning, including fostering his interest in numbers and books.

Moving on up

At just three years old, George moved to the 'threes to fives', a new part of the building for him, with new staff. Careful introduction to the new setting was planned for George and others who were transferring at the same time. This entailed frequent short visits and a transition summary which noted his interests and strengths as well as need for support. His profile books moved with him, providing a key emotional link for him, as well as information for his new key worker.

His mother noted on the Parents' Voice form how the profile book in itself has become a learning opportunity for him:

'He now has a good concept of what the profile book is and . . . realises that what he says gets written down. He sometimes asks us to write things so he can see what it looks like written down. George is starting to recognise some letters and numbers, often recognising the letters from his name. . . . his interests are still books and being read to – if he knows the story he likes to tell it with me. I am happy with George's progression in everything and that his key workers encourage him.'

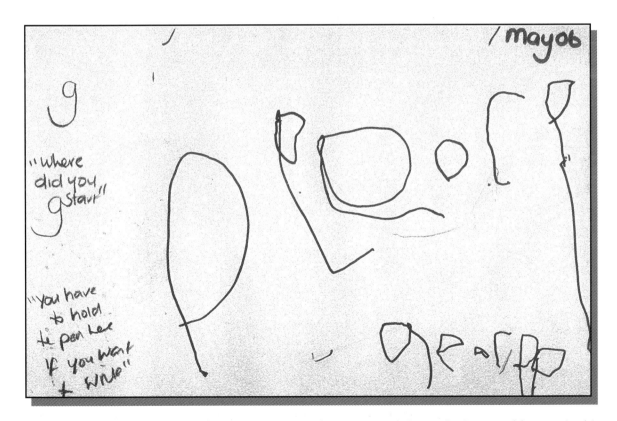

Fig. 8.5 At age 4 years 2 months, George's interest in writing continues: he is now able to write his full name, but still needs a little help with letter formation for lowercase 'g'.

And on to school . . .

When he was 4 years 10 months, George moved on to a local primary school. The transition was carefully planned to ensure he was familiar with the new environment, staff and routines. As before, his mother wrote about his latest interests in, for example, *'climbing – he will attempt almost anything . . .'* and *'he likes animals, creature and insect books . . . as well as Power Rangers and Dr Who. He is still confident and independent and wants to help with the cooking.'*

The nursery produces a summary report to go to the school: they call this a 'Passport'. It is produced on the computer using PowerPoint, containing photographs and a short statement about the child's development in each area of learning.

His new teacher found the information about the children, along with the visits the children do before they start, useful in helping her get to know them. She is well aware of George's interests and skills as he moves into the final half-term of his time in Reception. *'We have been studying minibeasts. I displayed some models of life cycles, such as the life cycle of a ladybird. George's observation skills are so well developed – he was in the small group of children who found a ladybird pupa and then some eggs in the garden – just from observing the large models we have in the classroom.'*

Summarising progress: from nursery setting to reception

Many local authorities provide transition records from nursery to reception class which consist of blank boxes for each area of learning, for staff to complete – summarising from the ongoing records, celebrating achievements and individuality, and also showing where the child needs further support – like the 'Passport' described above. This, I believe, is the best approach, respecting and valuing the child's personal achievements, so carefully documented through the observations and other evidence which have been collected. To make it come alive, real examples of special achievements, the child's own comment and those of parents should be used. Many include a drawing by the child too.

A smooth-running system will have been created, so long as the records for each child are regularly reviewed and learning priorities highlighted, keeping track of progress and feeding planning to ensure the child's learning is supported. Ongoing records, summarised from time to time, will ensure children's progress is tracked *against their own previous developments*, and planned for through the planning cycle as shown in Chapter 3. This will have documented the child's learning in the best possible way. As the EYFS (3.2 card) states: *'Every child's learning takes a personal path. . . .'*

Local authorities have a duty to ensure consistency through 'moderating' schools judgements in the EYFS Profile and an increasing number are beginning to moderate nursery settings too. Not only does this verify judgements in the summative transition records which are passed on, ensuring schools make use of them, but also it is supportive to the nursery settings, helping them in writing summaries and making secure judgements about children's progress.

Learning maps and other tracks for three to fives

In the EYFS, most of the Stepping Stones are contained in the later age bands of Development Matters, with a few additional statements added in some areas of learning. There are also, of course, all the statements referring to younger children in the earlier overlapping age bands. Increasingly, practitioners in the Foundation Stage – before the introduction of the EYFS – felt under pressure to produce a checklist as a tracking device, usually using Stepping Stones and Early Learning Goals. Many local authorities produced a format in this way, expecting their settings and school to use it. The real danger is that this becomes an alternative to good-quality formative assessment. This was not the purpose of the Stepping Stones and this is definitely *not* promoted in the EYFS, which explicitly states (Practice Guidance, p. 11) they **'. . . should not be used as checklists'**.

For those who feel they need some kind of tracking device when summarising ongoing records, and for transition records, perhaps the best way forward is to do what the practitioners in the Bond Primary School Foundation Stage Unit have done (see page 101). They created their own system for tracking progress for the three to five year olds, using more than the Stepping Stones (now in *Development Matters*), Early Learning Goals and Profile statements. But they do *not* do this at the expense of observing and making assessments from their observations. The 'learning map' tracking can only ever be an approximation of the child's actual development.

In Hutchin (2003), one teacher described her 'learning map' and how she created it, using her knowledge of child development and other curriculum documents such as the New Zealand curriculum *Te Whariki*, in addition to the Stepping Stones and Early Learning Goals, to create a more comprehensive picture. This is used for long-term planning, but also as a *guide* to assessment. The map is used to support practitioners in interpreting their judgements, which they then use for planning.

The Early Years Foundation Stage Profile

At the end of the EYFS is the first statutory assessment: the EYFS Profile. This is the official summative assessment for this phase in a child's education, and is only applicable to children in the final school year of the phase. It is entirely based on the previous Foundation Stage Profile, in methodology as well as content. Only two statements have been amended in line with new thinking about the teaching of literacy, in the Linking Sounds and Letters scale. The methodology is entirely consistent with the approach taken throughout this book to gathering evidence of children's learning.

How does the Profile work?

There are 13 nine-point scales, and within each there are three progressive bands. The first band comprises statements 1–3, at 'Stepping Stones' level: the statements from which they are compiled are now in the EYFS Development Matters, before the Early Learning Goals. The statements in the second band (statements 4–8) are taken from the Early Learning Goals. Point 9 in every scale describes a child who is working *beyond* the level of the Early Learning Goals. In order to be assessed at point 9, *all* of points 1–8 in the scale must have been achieved. In some cases, the statements for point 9 and some of the Early Learning Goal statements link closely to level 2 of the National Curriculum – for example in maths and literacy – although most are more closely linked to level 1 (Birmingham City Council, *Making Links*).

Many of the points in the scales are not hierarchical – i.e. they do not go from less to more advanced skills – but focus on different aspects of development within the area of learning concerned: see page 6 for details of the thirteen scales.

How are the assessments to be made?

Teachers are asked to make a judgement against each of the statements in the Profile, in June of their final year in the EYFS, before they enter Year 1. The judgements are based entirely on the ongoing records, the observations, views of parents and the child's view, as outlined here, along with other contributions such as from previous settings and any specialists involved. Transition records from previous settings are particularly important for children who move into reception in January or after Easter, as the judgements *'should represent your assessment of the child's typical attainment'*.

There are 117 statements altogether and in most cases they are broad summary statements. One reception teacher said: *'It isn't about the number of statements. It's about the records you keep. 117 statements are no problem, if you are carrying out observations, as most observations will tell you something about lots of the statements. You don't really need to spend much time making the final judgements.'*

Fig. 8.6

In Figure 8.6, Savannah (whose representation of development and growth appeared at the beginning of the chapter) is holding up a painting of a rainbow. Through regularly being involved in self-assessment, Savannah is able to express her views on her achievements. At 5 years and 2 months, this was what she felt was her best achievement in her school special folder.

Tracking progress through the year in reception

If a system of regular reviews, discussions with parents and conferences with the child has been established, completing the Profile should be relatively easy and not too time-consuming. Having reviewed the record and set appropriate learning priorities or targets regularly through the EYFS phase, as described in Chapter 6, this will be the ideal opportunity for reception teachers to make a summative assessment in line with the EYFS Profile.

Many local authorities and settings prefer that the Stepping Stones (now in later parts of the Development Matters section) are used, for good reason. The Profile has condensed the Stepping Stones into three statements per scale, whereas some areas of learning had many more – Knowledge and Understanding of the World (KUW) had 28 in all, while Number as Labels and for Counting had 20! Whichever you use, the important thing to decide is: *What has the child achieved?* There are likely to be some gaps – for example in a particular scale where no evidence has yet been recorded. But tracking development once per term in this way is likely to make the task of completing it at the end of the year much less onerous.

Making use of the EYFSP in Year 1

Although the Profile marks the official end of the assessment process for the EYFS period, there is little point in it unless the information gathered can be *used* to ensure planning is right for the child in Year 1. It may be a summative assessment, but it must be *used* in a formative way. The importance of the Profile as a summative assessment is that it is so comprehensive, covering the full range of learning, not just of the curriculum on offer in the final year of the phase, but more holistically – of child development. With such a full picture of the child's achievements, it lends itself easily to being used for planning.

However, perhaps due to the differences in approach and terminology in the National Curriculum, it has taken a long time to embed the proper use of the Profile for informing planning in

Year 1. In 2005 the QCA produced a folder of training materials entitled *Continuing the Learning Journey*. This focused on how to make use of the information and data which could be generated from the FS Profile at school level, to look for patterns in achievements across the scales and the group of children. The materials apply equally to the EYFS Profile, and are highly recommended. However, the most important aspect is using the information to ensure that the individual children are properly catered for.

A classful of children may have vastly different achievements in any one particular scale. Two children may attain the same score, but the actual statements they achieve may be very different. Figure 8.7 gives an example from the Reading scale which illustrates this point:

Reading

Scale point	EYFS Profile Scale statement	Child A	Child B
1	*Is developing an interest in books*	✓	✓
2	*Knows that print conveys meaning*	✓	✓
3	*Recognises a few familiar words*		✓
4	*Knows that in English print is read from left to right and top to bottom*	✓	✓
5	*Shows an understanding of the elements of stories, such as main character, sequence of events and openings*	✓	✓
6	*Reads a range of familiar and common words and simple sentences independently*		✓
7	*Retells narratives in the correct sequence, drawing on language patterns of stories*	✓	
8	*Shows an understanding of how information can be found in non-fiction texts to answer questions about where, who, why and how*	✓	
9	*Reads books of own choice with some fluency and accuracy*		
TOTAL		**6**	**6**

Fig. 8.7

Points for reflection

- How do you ensure continuity in children's learning and development through their various transitions to/from your own setting, such as from home to your setting and from your setting to the next?

- How do you track children's progress in your setting? Does it ensure that every child's unique learning journey is valued and documented?

Managing the processes

9

The observation, assessment and planning *cycle* is vital to supporting every child's learning and development. For some settings and practitioners, this cycle is well-established practice. Where this is so, they have ensured that all other systems and routines support this process to make sure it works. Other settings and practitioners, however, have expressed concerns about how to make this manageable. There is practical advice throughout this book, but getting the processes to work *effectively* has implications for how the day is organised, the type of learning environment you have set up and, most of all, how practitioners work with the children. This is the focus of this chapter. Managing effective systems requires a commitment to being flexible and confident to try out changes on the basis of continually evaluating existing practice.

Managing change to support learning and development

Self-evaluation and reflection

What children can learn and how they develop is totally dependent on what is provided and the way in which this is presented to the children. What we celebrate, allow, condone or condemn moulds our practice. As Lancaster (2006) warns us: *'Our taken-for-granted views about children and childhood have the potential to hinder children from actually achieving the outcomes we are working towards.'* Evaluating practice is essential to ensure planning, pedagogy and provision are not limited by the established status quo.

Self-evaluation has been a significant aspect of the formal inspection process since 2005, with schools and settings expected to review their own strengths and areas for development. It allows us to celebrate success. Observations of the children and how they use the provision made available to them is often the best way to evaluate that provision. There are many ways of evaluating practice, but here are two which are particularly helpful. They focus on evaluating *processes and practice* rather than outcomes, which is discussed in relation to using data from the EYFS Profile, described in Chapter 8.

An action research model

Action research has a long-established tradition within education, and many programmes and projects in early childhood provision use this approach to develop practice. To understand the processes involved, the order of the words needs reversing: the first part of the process is to *research* an aspect of your provision or practice to find out what is currently happening, and the second part is to take *action* as a result of what you found out. Every future action is further evaluated or 'researched'. Some 'quality improvement' schemes such as *Effective Early Learning* use a highly effective action research model following a structured process. But it is also something that can be done by one practitioner – or, better still, in a setting or school, with the whole team – in a less prescriptive way.

Researching our own practice can be an exciting process of investigation through observing children, observing how staff interact with the children, and how the children use the provision, as well as practitioners' views and parents' views. Sharing the knowledge gained between the team can re-enthuse the whole team into wanting to develop practice. Other questions are important too. What does research tell us? What do we think we *should* be doing? What do others think?

'The cycle of informed reflection, self-evaluation and development that lies at the heart of the process takes time, openness and the capacity to step back and look at your practice with absolute honesty – warts and all!' (Jaeckle, 2006). However, it is well worth doing. Sometimes a child or parent's comment can get you started. For me, on one occasion it was sparked off by two boys telling me they *should* be able to use the wheel toys, even though it was a 'girls-only day', as the girls were not using them. That got me thinking: *'Why don't the girls use the wheel toys in spite of all our efforts?'* This became my 'research' question.

A quick review of an area of practice

Once the processes of reflection and self-evaluation are a firmly established aspect of the setting or school's practice, a quick review can often result in developing more effective ways of working. Some possible areas for review may be:

- If observing is felt to be onerous work by some members of the staff team, what is it they are observing and how do they make use of their observations?
- If there are very few observations in a particular area of learning, how much emphasis is there on this area of learning, especially within play?
- Why is it that there are very few observations on some children but lots on others? Is it because adults rarely get involved in the aspect of provision which really interests these children?

A quick check (for example, over one or two sessions) looking at the aspect of provision highlighted for attention can often be very revealing. The important thing is to decide, as a team, what to do to improve it, remembering that the actions taken are not necessarily quick fixes: they need time to plan, get started, embed into practice, review and evaluate.

Learning environments that inspire

The environment is such a powerful teacher. An inspiring, vibrant and well-organised learning environment supports learning: a dull, ill-thought-out or sterile learning environment does not. If it is rich and stimulating, arousing curiosity and interest, play is where children will operate at their highest cognitive level. The best form of support for children's learning – where sustained shared thinking is most likely to happen – is within a rich, enabling environment, when practitioners support children in their child-initiated learning (Siraj-Blatchford et al, 2002 – see chapter 2). And most importantly, a well-managed environment frees staff from managerial tasks, enabling them to get involved in supporting and extending learning and to observe whilst they work with the children.

Outdoor environments

6 *Being outdoors . . . offers opportunities for doing things in different ways and on different scales than when indoors. It gives children first-hand contact with weather, seasons and the natural world and offers children freedom to explore, use their senses, and be physically active and exuberant.* 9 (EYFS card 3.3)

As Angela, a teacher in one of the case studies, said, *'Outdoor play can be the best place to observe children at play'*, but to be able to see children operating at their highest level and to carry out observations effectively, the provision must be engaging – motivating children to explore, investigate, imagine and practise their skills.

For the youngest children

In creating the environment, practitioners will need to consider:
- Does the environment and layout support the development of positive relationships – with comfortable, cosy spaces to sit for adults and the babies and toddlers?
- Does the environment encourage the children and babies to experiment, try things out and often be messy? Are there plenty of natural materials, of different textures and different sizes and shapes? Are there materials to explore, such as water, sand, cornflour gloop and paint? Have resources been set out in such a way that the babies and youngest toddlers can explore with their bodies, rather than with tools such as brushes or spades? Are there treasure baskets and heuristic play sessions? (Goldschmied and Jackson, 1994)
- What materials and encouragements are provided to develop the children's creativity?
- Are the spaces light, airy and calm?
- Are there suitable physical challenges, such as different surfaces for crawling and walking on? Is climbing available at the appropriate level of difficulty to enable safe risk-taking?
- For toddlers, is there provision for role play, including home-corner resources and dressing-up?
- How does the environment meet the principles and commitments of the EYFS?

Twos to fives

For older children, the best way is to set up areas of provision or 'learning bays' (Bilton, 1998) which will make sense to the children and to the staff. For example, areas which should always be available are: role play, small world play, construction, creative (or designing and making) workshop, sand, water and malleable play, an investigation and exploration area, a quiet area to think, feel and be, a graphics area, a book area, art area and stimuli available to encourage children to use of these. Outside should be similar but on a larger scale. Childminders will be providing the same at home for this age group – not simultaneously, but over time. This is, of course, only part of the story. It will not be rich and stimulating unless it also enables children to celebrate and share their experiences of their own cultures, languages and heritages.

Providing a stimulating environment means not just making the provision available, but showing we value it. The amount of status given to the sand play, for example, is perhaps most easily noted by the amount of time staff spend there, as well as how well organised the resources are. Wherever possible, involve the children in reviewing the environment – what do *they* think needs improving? Using the approaches mentioned in Chapter 5 will help, particularly accessing the views of younger children (Lancaster, 2003; Clark and Moss, 2001).

This is the way the learning environment was set up in the Foundation Stage Unit in the case study (page 101). Although this environment was created for children from three, much of this is equally applicable to two year olds.

The Unit consists of a large, open-planned area, organised into learning bays or areas of provision, such as creative, exploration and investigation, and spaces for quieter activities, construction, sand and water in copious quantities with well organised resources and small-group, table-based activities. There are several imaginative play locations and roleplay areas, as well as book corners.

The environment reflects and celebrates the cultures and languages in the local community and the multi-ethnic nature of society. The outdoor area, a fenced, asphalted section of the school playground, provides a wealth of opportunities across the areas of learning including large construction, role play, gardening, music, drama and creative arts, as well as physical development.

Accessibility of resources and use of space

Across the age range, resources and equipment need to be accessible to the children: not too little and not too much, with as many natural materials as possible, support multi-sensory learning. Storage needs to be clearly labelled (in pictures and words) and well organised. Very little needs to be expensive – the most useful and 'educational' are open-ended resources, such as wooden blocks, and those that encourage cooperation, such as carts and taxi-bikes. So much can be done with safe 'reclaimed materials' such as boxes, packaging, 'scrap store' materials – which, like other resources, should always be checked for safety and appropriateness. What matters is the display and presentation of materials and resources – what Pat Gura (1996) calls *'stuff'* – and, above all, what we *allow* the children to do with the 'stuff' which is as important as the 'stuff' itself.

Maintaining the environment

'Maintaining our learning environment takes a lot of work', the staff in the Foundation Stage Unit told me *'but it is well worth doing. Children learn so much from the environment, but they have to know how to use it. Attention to detail is incredibly important – like having an interactive display on the wall in the corridor children walk down when they get their coats or go to the toilets. It is there for them to look at and interact with – all times of day are times for learning. We have a learning environment where children help themselves to the resources they need. We don't plan in advance what we will be putting out on the tables, but track what happened afterwards, by writing it up in the daily evaluation. It works because we are tight on routines and procedures: this allows us to be flexible.'*

Keeping it tidy

The next thing is to ensure the children are trained not only to use the environment and the resources, but also to *put things away* when they have finished. Good procedures for tidying-up are essential if the environment is to be maintained. It is worth sharing what the Unit did with ninety children, all in one environment. They told me:

'Tidying-up procedures are vital if this is going to work. So we have done it this way: reception children are assigned an area of the room (such as construction or book area or role play) which they are always responsible for tidying. Nursery children help them and help the adults, but are not assigned the responsibility. Children are **trained** *how to tidy the area and, because they are there every day, they know it well and develop a sense of pride in it. We have given them a sense of ownership of the environment, helping them to take responsibility.'*

Two really useful guides to developing the learning environments are *A Place to Learn* (LEARN, 2002) and *Learning Outdoors* (Bilton et al, 2005).

Fig. 9.1 Children in the Foundation Stage Unit take pride in keeping their environment tidy

Adult deployment: who does what, where, when?

The well-managed learning environment enables children to learn effectively so long as the adults use it effectively too. This means coordinating the staff team to ensure they are fully involved in supporting the children.

What should the adult role look like across the age range?

The *key person* role is now statutory in the Early Years Foundation Stage for good reason: babies and young children need to make close emotional attachments in order to feel secure and grow up confident and self-assured.

> *Even when children are older [in the EYFS years] there is still a need for them to have a key person to depend on in the setting such as their teacher or teaching assistant.* (EYFS 2.4)

There is very helpful information on the EYFS CD-ROM 'in depth' about the significance of the key person and how to manage the role.

With children under three, the key person is the most important aspect of adult deployment. For settings which are all-year-round, with staff on shifts, the EYFS advises that each child should have a second key person (often called a co-key worker) so that holidays and shifts are covered by one other person the child knows well. With children from three, the key person role is still fundamental for developing secure relationships, settling-in new children and providing the link with parents. They also have the responsibility for keeping observations and record-keeping up to date for their key children.

Beyond these basic responsibilities, the day-to-day roles of the staff need careful planning to ensure that while one member of staff is involved in a planned activity, others are interacting and working with the children in their play and self-chosen activities. In both roles, observing is an integral part of the work, jotting quick notes on self-adhesive labels or Post-its at the time. It is important that roles are shared, to ensure all staff have an opportunity to be involved in supporting play as well as carrying out focused, adult-framed activities. Finally, a staff member involved in play will often be the one to carry out any planned, focused observation on a child, timetabled into the day.

Organising routines and time

Routines can sometimes inadvertently hinder children's learning – for example, by frequently interrupting the children to move to another part of the setting or join a group time in the middle of a session. Are the sessions planned to maximise children's deep involvement in what they are doing? Is time spent on managerial-type tasks and routines kept to a minimum? For example, from the age of two or three, at the beginning of the day, children should be able to 'self-register' with their name labels and the help of a parent, after which they then go straight to an activity of their own choosing – enabling practitioners to talk to parents, settle any child who needs it, and support children in their free choices. This not only ensures children's time is spent engaged in active learning, rather than just waiting for something to happen, but helps build relationships with parents.

Organising time

Observing, assessing and compiling records should be seen as part of the role of the practitioner during the daytime, not at the end of the day when children have gone. One observation of a child deeply involved in play will usually provide a great deal of evidence in several aspects of learning and development. Once practitioners understand how to make assessments from observations, in the ways described in Chapter 4, the majority of these can be made at the time the observation is carried out. Compiling the records into individual folders with the children provides some very valuable learning, giving them the chance to discuss and reflect on what they have been doing. It also boosts self-esteem and begins the process of self-reflection.

Making the most of the available time is one of the big issues, especially in full day-care settings. Where there are younger children, how are sleep times used? In settings with younger children, use the time when children sleep to have planning meetings with some staff whilst others supervise the sleepers. As Caron in Fortune Park said: *'Time management is crucial. We need to ensure staff are flexible and use every minute so there is no time wasting – if there are fewer children in one day, then a member of staff can be asked to do some development work on something else.'*

In the Foundation Stage Unit, to maximise time, the daily evaluation is done at the end of the day: *'Our daily evaluation is a really important part of the planning process. As we are tidying-up every day, we discuss a variety of aspects of the day and it takes anything from 3 or 4 minutes to 15 minutes. Sometimes we also need to meet and talk at lunchtime too.'*

Are all parents involved?

Effective links with parents was discussed in Chapter 5. If all parents are going to be fully included in finding out about their children's day-to-day life in the setting, then routines of the day must ensure that staff have time to talk to them. But some parents do not pick up their own children and rarely get to see their child's key person. Ways of communicating with them need to be developed. The EYFS emphasises the need for continuity for *children* between settings, and the same is true for *parents*: for a three to five year old who is in an 'after-school' setting at the end of the day and a 'breakfast club' at the beginning, parents will have little contact with the school. The same is true for children (often disabled children) who make the journey between home and school on a school bus. There are many effective ways that settings and schools have bridged this gap – simple daily diaries, regular telephone or email contact – but this cannot replace the face-to-face conversation. Arranging parent consultations at times which suit parents best is vital.

Continuity

Continuity across settings is crucial, particularly when a child attends more than one setting. It has become a statutory requirement in the EYFS that *'practitioners must ensure continuity and coherence'*. Links between private and voluntary-sector early years providers and schools have been significantly strengthened over recent years, thanks to local authority early years training. In most areas there are joint training sessions and local meetings, and practitioners are encouraged to use similar record-keeping formats. But making your own personal links, through arranging visits to each other's settings within your locality and getting to know how each other works, will be the best way of supporting continuity for the children.

Meeting professional development needs

Sharing ideas with others and attending regular professional development is also vital in developing practice and sustaining change. There has been a significant emphasis on professional development and raising the level of qualifications in the early childhood workforce in recent years. This is to be heartily welcomed, ensuring the practitioners attend the right courses to develop their particular professional skills.

In the reception year, training and informing new staff may be a challenge. Both teachers and support staff often change the age group they work with. There are also those joining the profession for the first time, so professional development is necessary. These issues may be equally applicable to nursery class staff. It is important that the whole staff team can train together. Increasingly, day nurseries are implementing a small number of whole-staff training days with the agreement of parents, and playgroups will use the school inservice training days for their own training and meetings too.

Just as important is ensuring that when staff members have attended training, they are given time to share what they have found out with others in their setting. This needs careful planning, particularly in a large primary school with a tight schedule of meetings booked well in advance, or in a large all-year-round day nursery or children's centre with few opportunities for staff meetings. Developing ways of feeding back by other means – such as using a bulletin board or a reminder book, where staff on the course are expected to write a quick synopsis and others sign when they have read it – will help. Then if comments are added by others who want to know more, the best way of disseminating the information – whether to a few or the whole team – can be decided by the team leaders and managers.

Points for reflection
- How do you maintain an inspiring learning environment where you and other staff can be fully involved in supporting every child's learning and development?
- What do you find the most effective way of evaluating your practice and developing it further?

Reflecting back and looking forward 10

In the Introduction, the point was made that our real accountability is to the children in our care, and we owe it to them to get the planning right. The aim of this book has been to help practitioners meet this challenge and ensure that *all* children's learning and development is supported by the settings they attend in the EYFS and as they continue into Year 1 in school. The central theme has been:

■ start with the children;
■ find out about their interests, concerns, achievements and learning needs;
■ tailor the learning opportunities you will offer next to what will suit them best.

This means beginning with observing the children, listening to their parents and others who know them well, listening to the children themselves and using all this as the basis for planning. But it also means being aware of diversity and difference between the children, being prepared to be inclusive and open-minded and, most of all, valuing every child as unique and special. This is not just about being open to individuality. Rinaldi (2001) talks about *'being open to the complex, conflictual and unpredictable nature of human learning wherever it takes place'*.

Continuity across the age range

Throughout the book I have demonstrated how the processes outlined above for observing, assessing and planning need to be essentially the same across the age range. In Chapter 3, these were portrayed in a diagram (Fig 3.1) called the *planning cycle*. This should be a continuous process through the various transitions and transfers children will encounter on the way. As discussed in Chapter 8, regular reviews and summaries support practitioners in planning, tracking progress and developing records to pass on at times of transition. Fig 10.1 shows how this system works, from the beginning of the EYFS phase to Year 1, in one continuing spiral.

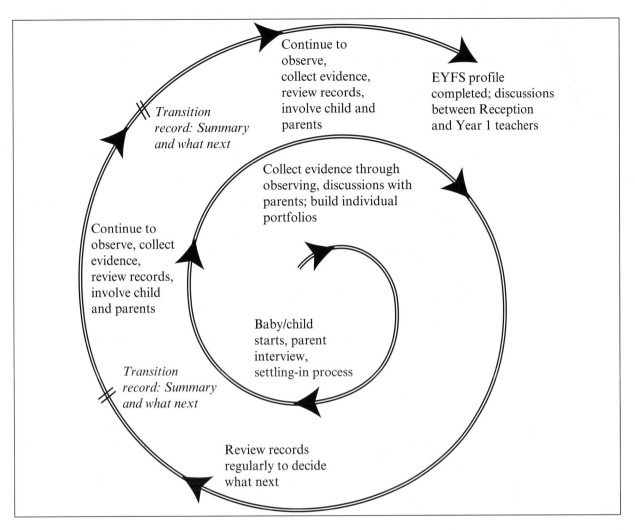

Fig. 10.1 *The 'progress and development' spiral*

Summing up

Looking back over the last nine chapters, the main messages have been:

- Ensure your vision for your setting is open and inclusive, based on high expectations of all children, and built on an understanding of how children learn and develop and the uniqueness of every child.
- Enable children to learn through play, supporting them to extend their relationships with others, their explorations, learning, thinking and self-esteem.

■ Find out about each child as an individual, their achievements, and their learning and development needs through partnership with parents and your observations.

■ Listen to the child's voice, and observe what interests them.

■ Document the children's learning, so that it celebrates all children's achievements and supports their future learning.

■ Once all the above are in place, start your short-term planning on the basis of what you found out.

■ Be reflective. Use the EYFS principles and commitments as well as the research findings and principles outlined in Chapters 2 and 3 as an opportunity to review your vision and practice.

Points for reflection

● How can you develop closer links with other settings so that your setting's assessment and planning processes contribute to the learning and development spiral for each child, outlined in Figure 10.1?

● Use the points summarised above to consider your setting's practice. Think about how parents could contribute further to your self-evaluation processes.

Last word

Finally, many children, parents, practitioners and teachers in a range of schools and settings, as well as a childminder at home, have helped me to write this book by providing the examples to illustrate the processes of observing, assessing, planning involving parents, and involving the children. Most of all, this book is about adults supporting children's learning and development by observing them, listening to them and taking time with them. Let us leave the last word to one child, Benjamin, now four and a half.

I asked him to tell me about himself. The discussion was introduced by his mother saying: 'We want to ask you some questions.'

Benjamin already knows a lot about questions, so he asked her the first question: 'What are you most scared of?' After she had answered I asked him the same question.

Benjamin: 'Earthquakes.'

Me: 'Why?'

Benjamin: 'I don't want to fall down the cracks . . . and hot lava . . . because it's hot.'

I think most of us would agree with Benjamin there – they are things to be taken very seriously!

Me: 'What do you like doing best of all?'

Benjamin: 'Driving a train.'

A conversation followed about **Thomas the Tank Engine** *and how he liked all the engines in the books 'except for diesels – they're mean.'*

He likes playing with his toy dinosaurs. He remembers visiting the museum (months before) and was very impressed by the big robot dinosaurs and especially 'T rex': 'It stares and then it runs! I ate a dinosaur pancake for breakfast – it was a triceratops'.

Another favourite at present is **Star Wars** *and 'lightsabers'. When he was asked what he liked doing best at nursery, he told me he liked playing 'lightsabers'.*

Children's burning concerns and passions must be considered – we need to find out what these are and make these the most important concern when planning. It will be different with different children and at different ages. For a great many three and four year olds, imagination and what we call 'fantasy play' are critically important in learning, supporting their development in all spheres: emotional, social, physical and cognitive. We cannot leave these on one side, if we really want to engage them. Observations will show that it is not the only thing they do, but to them it is the most important! Benjamin is able to articulate his passions and concerns clearly through words. Other children will not yet be able to do this, and, for some, communication of any kind may always be a struggle – which makes observation and the processes for listening to children outlined in Chapter 5 even more important.

Vivian Gussin Paley, in her book *A Child's Work* (2004), refers to play as *children's work*. As in most of her writings, she focuses on helping us to understand the vital importance of imagination and fantasy play to young children: *'Fantasy play, rather than being a distraction, helps children to achieve the goal of having an open mind, whether in the service of further story telling or in formal lessons.'*

My last question to Benjamin was: 'Is there anything you wish you could do but you can't quite manage yet?'

Benjamin: 'Drive a train.'

As he grows older, his own aspirations for himself will change and develop, but at the moment the fantastic world of books, films and cartoons which fire the imagination alongside factual knowledge, is his current burning concern. He also draws and paints, runs and climbs, like most other children of his age. In Figure 10.2, he has drawn his family and his dog, and – as you can see – he is already beginning to write.

Fig. 10.2 Benjamin's family

References

Official Publications

England:

DfES (2007) *Early Years Foundation Stage* pack

The pack can be ordered from DfES publications, PO Box 5050, Sherwood Park, Annesley, Nottinghamshire NG15 0DJ Tel: 0845 60 22260, fax: 0845 60 333 60.

The EYFS pack is made up of the Statutory Framework and Practice Guidance booklets, Principles into Practice cards, Wall Poster and CD-ROM. It is available to download from two websites: www.everychildmatters.gov.uk and www.teachernet.gov.uk/publications .

A wide variety of documents relevant to early childhood education and care are on the CD-ROM. Many of these have been referred to in the text of this book – such as the *Birth to Three Literature Review* (2003) and REPEY.

DfES (2006a) *Early Years Foundation Stage consultation on a single quality framework for services for children birth to five,* available for download on www.teachernet.gov.uk/publications

DfES (2003) *Birth to Three Matters Framework.*

DfES (2004) *Social and Emotional Aspects of Learning materials,* available on website:

DfES (2006b), *Personal Social and Emotional Development: Training Materials, birth to five.* www.standards.dfes.gov.uk/primary/publications/banda/seal/

DfES (2006c) *2020 Vision: Report of the Teaching and Learning in 2020 Review Group,* www.teachernet.gov.uk/publications

DfES (2007) *Improving the use of ICT in the Foundation Stage,* http://www.standards.dfes.gov.uk/primary/casestudies/

HM Treasury (2004) *Choice for parents, the best start for children,* available for download on www.everychildmatters.gov.uk

National Assessment Agency (NAA) publishes a range of additional guidance on the Foundation Stage Profile and EYFS Profile, website address: www.naa.org.uk

Ofsted (2007) *The Foundation Stage: A Report of 144 Settings,* HMI 2610, available on www.ofsted.gov.uk

QCA/DfES (2000) *Curriculum Guidance for the Foundation Stage.*

QCA (2005) *Continuing the Learning Journey.*

SCAA (1997) *Looking at Children's Learning.*

New Zealand: *Te Whariki: Early Childhood Curriculum* (1996) New Zealand Ministry of Education, Wellington: Learning Media.

Northern Ireland: *Curricular Guidance for Pre-school Education* (no date), Northern Ireland Department for Education. More information on the website: www.deni.gov.uk

Scotland: Learning and Teaching Scotland (2005) *Birth to Three: Supporting Our Youngest Children*, Edinburgh, HMSO.

Scottish Office (2006) *A Curriculum for Excellence*, appendices to proposals.

Wales: information about the Foundation Phase and *A Flying Start* in Wales can be obtained from www.new.wales.gov.uk

(See also Davidson, J., references below.)

Early Childhood Research

Sylva, K., Melhuish, E. C., Sammons, P., Siraj-Blatchford, I. and Taggart, B. (2004) *The Effective Provision of Pre-School Education (EPPE) Project: Technical Paper 12 – The Final Report: Effective Pre-School Education.* London: DfES/Institute of Education, University of London.

Sylva, K., Melhuish, E. C., Sammons, P., Siraj-Blatchford, I. and Taggart, B. (2007) Effective Pre-school and Primary Education, EPPE 3–11 http://www.ioe.ac.uk/schools/ecpe/eppe/

Melhuish, E. C, Quinn, L., Hanna, K., Sylva, K., Sammons, P., Siraj-Blatchford, I. and Taggart, B. (2006) *The Effective Pre-School Provision in Northern Ireland [EPPNI] Project Summary report, 1998–2004.*

Siraj-Blatchford, I., Sylva, K., et al (2002) *Researching Effective Pedagogy in the Early Years (REPEY)*, DfES.

Early Childhood Education and Child Development

Assessment Reform Group (1999) *Assessment for Learning: Beyond the Black Box*, University of Cambridge School of Education.

Assessment Reform Group (2002) *Assessment for Learning: Ten Principles*, www.assessment-reform-group.org.uk

Bath Spa University, Penny Hale and Julia Butler (2002, ongoing) *5×5×5 Creativity, Researching Children Researching the World*, contact: info5×5×5@btinternet.com

Bertram, T. and Pascal, C. (2004) *Effective Early Learning Programme. Evaluating and Improving Quality in Early childhood Settings: A Professional Improvement Programme*, University College Worcester.

Bertram, T. and Pascal, C. (2006) 'Introducing Child Development', in Bruce, T., *Early Childhood, a Guide for Students*, Sage Publications.

Bertram, T. and Pascal, C. (2007) *Baby Effective Early Learning Programme. Evaluating and Improving Quality in Early childhood Settings: A Professional Improvement Programme*, University College Worcester.

Birmingham City Council (no date) *Supporting Transition from the Foundation Stage to Key Stage 1: Making Links.*

Bilton, H.. (1998) *Outdoor Play in the Early Years: Management and Innovation*, David Fulton.

Bilton, H., James, K., Marsh, J., Wilson, A., Woonton, M. (2005) *Learning Outdoors: improving the quality of young children's play outdoors*, David Fulton.

Black, P. and Wiliam, D. (1998) *Inside the Black Box: Raising Standards through Classroom Assessment*, Kings College, London, Dept of Education and Professional Studies.

Boyd Cadwell, L. (1997) *Bringing Reggio Emilia Home*, Teachers College Press, Columbia University.

Brown, B. (1998) *Unlearning Discrimination in the Early Years*, Trentham Books.

Bruce, T. (2004) *Cultivating Creativity in Babies, Toddlers and Young Children*, Hodder.

Bruner, J. (1981) 'What is representation?' In Roberts, M. and Tamburrini, J. (eds) *Child Development 0–5*, Holmes Mcdougill.

Carr, M. (2001) *Assessment in Early Childhood Settings: Learning Stories, Effective Early Learning*, Paul Chapman Publishing.

Carr, M., Jones, C., and Lee, W. (2005) 'Beyond listening: can assessment practice play a part?' in Clark, A., Kjorholt, A.T., and Moss, P., *Beyond Listening: children's perspectives on early childhood services* , The Policy Press, University of Bristol.

Clark, A., and Moss, P. (2001) *Listening to Young Children: The Mosiac Approach*, National Children's Bureau and Joseph Rowntree Foundation.

Coram Family (2003) *'Listening to Young Children' pack*, Open University Press.

Cousins , J. (1999) *Listening to Four Year Olds*, National Early Years Network.

Davidson, Jane (adapted from a speech at the Aspect Conference June 2006) 'A Foundation Phase for Wales', *Early Education, 51*, Spring 2007.

Driscoll,V. and Rudge,C. (2005) 'Channels for listening to young children and parents', in Clark, A., Kjorholt, A.T., and Moss, P., *Beyond Listening: children's perspectives on early childhood services* , The Policy Press, University of Bristol.

Drummond, M. J. (1993) *Assessing Children's Learning*, David Fulton.

Duffy, B. (1998) *Supporting Creativity and Imagination in the Early Years*, Open University Press.

Fisher, J. (1998) *Starting with the Child*, Open University Press.

Gardner, H. (1999) *Intelligence Reframed*, Basic Books.

Goleman, D. (1996) *Emotional Intelligence*, Bloomsbury.

Goldshmied, E. and Jackson, S. (1994) *People Under Three: Young Children in Day Care*, Routledge.

Gura, P. (1996) *Resources for Early Learning: Children, Adults and Stuff*, Hodder.

Gura, P., and Hall, L. (2000) 'Self assessment', in *Early Years Educator*, June 2000, Mark Allen Publishing.

Hutchin, V. (1999) *Right from the Start: Effective Planning and Assessment in the Early Years*, Hodder.

Hutchin, V. (2003) *Observing and Assessing for the Foundation Stage Profile*, Hodder.

Hutchin, V. (2006) 'Meeting Individual Needs', in Bruce, T., *Early Childhood, a Guide for Students*, Sage Publications.

Jaeckle, S. (2006) 'Managing Yourself and your Learning', in Bruce, T., *Early Childhood, a Guide for Students*, Sage Publications.

Jarman, E. (2006) *Communication-Friendly Spaces*, Basic Skills Agency, www.basic-skills.co.uk

Laevers, F. (2002) *Research on Experiential Education Reader: A selection of articles by Ferre Laevers*, Centre for Experiential Education, Leuven.

Lancaster, Y. P. (2003) *Promoting Listening to Young Children: The Reader*, Open University Press.

Lancaster, Y. P. (2006) 'Listening to Young Children, Respecting the Voice of the Child', in Pugh, G., and Duffy, B., *Contemporary Issues in the Early Years*, fourth edition, Sage Publications.

Lewisham Early Years Advice and Resource Network (2002) *A Place to Learn*, tel: 020 8695 9806; eys.advisers@lewisham.gov.uk

Malaguzzi, L (1993) 'No way – the hundred is there', in Edwards, C., Gandini, L. and Forman, G. (Eds) *The Hundred Languages of Children: the Reggio Emilia approach to early childhood education*, Norwood, NJ: Ablex Publishing.
Further information and references can be obtained from the website: www.reggiochildren.it

Nutbrown, C. (1994) *Threads of Thinking*, Paul Chapman Publishing.

Paley, V. G. (1990) *The Boy Who would Be a Helicopter: the uses of storytelling in the classroom*, Harvard University Press.

Paley, V. G. (2004) *A Child's Work: the Importance of Fantasy Play*, University of Chicago Press.

Rinaldi, C. (2001) 'Infant Toddler Centers and Pre-schools as Places of Cutlure', in Giudici, C., Rinaldi, C.,and Krechevsky, M., *Making Learning Visible: children as individual and group learners*, Reggio Children, Italy

Rinaldi, C. (2005) 'Documentation and Assessment: what is the relationship?', in Clark, A., Kjorholt, A.T., and Moss, P., *Beyond Listening: children's perspectives on early childhood services* , The Policy Press, University of Bristol.

Vygotsky, L. (1978) *Mind in Society*, Harvard University Press.

Wells, G. (1986) *The Meaning Makers: Children Learning language and Using Language to Learn*, Hodder.

Wood, D. (1998) *How Children Think and Learn*, Blackwell.

1

7 DAY
BOOK